Praise for Conflicted Scars

"I loved playing in the OHL, the second-best league in the world, and I have loved my life in the NHL. Justin's book should be on the shelf of every hockey parent. He has some amazing stories . . . and every former player will vouch for them. Canada loves hockey, and rightly so, but we have to make sure the kids come first. I am glad my friend wrote this book." — Joe Thornton, 22-year NHL veteran and Hart Memorial and Art Ross Trophy winner

"Justin Davis shows us that hockey is a lot like life. It can be glorious. It can be painful. You can fall in love one moment and be heartbroken the next. This book is a must-read for anyone who ever dreamed of playing in the NHL, or perhaps more importantly, for any parent who is dreaming that their child could be The Next One." — Ken Reid, Sportsnet Central Host and best-selling author of *Hockey Card Stories*

"Justin Davis blows the doors off all your assumptions about Junior hockey. He courageously reevaluates the toxic culture he was a part of and what was considered to be normal rites of passage and team-bonding by everyone involved in the sport. *Conflicted Scars* is essential reading for all hockey fans and an important contribution to exposing the dark underbelly of the game that has been kept secret for far too long." — Allan Walsh, Player Agent

"Honest, sometimes uncomfortable storytelling makes this a must-read for every parent whose child is chasing the all-too-familiar dream of becoming a professional hockey player. Multiple *Are you kidding me?* moments. I couldn't put it down." — Rick Westhead, Senior Correspondent at TSN Sports and CTV National News

"In hockey, we celebrate the stories of the stars that play the game and glorify the scars that come with it. This book uncovers the internal scars players face long-term and their struggles to figure out right and wrong. Justin Davis has lived and breathed the game and its many nuances and contradictions. He beautifully captures why the sport leaves so many with those conflicted scars." — James Duthie, award-winning host of TSN Hockey and bestselling author of *The Guy on the Left*

CONFLICTED
SCARS

CONFLICTED
SCARS

AN
AVERAGE
PLAYER'S
JOURNEY
TO THE NHL

JUSTIN DAVIS

Published by ECW Press
665 Gerrard Street East
Toronto, Ontario, Canada M4M 1Y2
416-694-3348 / info@ecwpress.com

Editor for the Press: Michael Holmes
Copy editor: Laura Pastore
Cover design: Michel Vrana

Reference used: Turnpenney, Rachel. (2022). *Report on the CHL's Player Wellbeing Programs and Related Recommendations*. Turnpenney Milne LLP. https://cdn.chl.ca/uploads/chl/2022/01/21095713/PlayerWellbeingUpdate_FINAL.pdf.

LIBRARY AND ARCHIVES CANADA CATALOGUING IN PUBLICATION

Title: Conflicted scars : an average player's journey to the NHL / Justin Davis.

Names: Davis, Justin, 1978- author.

Identifiers: Canadiana (print) 20220248249 | Canadiana (ebook) 20220248362

ISBN 978-1-77041-623-9 (softcover)
ISBN 978-1-77852-005-1 (ePub)
ISBN 978-1-77852-006-8 (PDF)
ISBN 978-1-77852-007-5 (Kindle)

Subjects: LCSH: Davis, Justin, 1978- | LCSH: Hockey players— Biography. | LCGFT: Autobiographies.

Classification: LCC GV848.5.D325 A3 2022 | DDC 796.962092—dc23

We acknowledge the support of the Canada Council for the Arts. *Nous remercions le Conseil des arts du Canada de son soutien.* This book is funded in part by the Government of Canada. *Ce livre est financé en partie par le gouvernement du Canada.* We acknowledge the support of the Ontario Arts Council (OAC), an agency of the Government of Ontario, which last year funded 1,965 individual artists and 1,152 organizations in 197 communities across Ontario for a total of $51.9 million. We also acknowledge the support of the Government of Ontario through the Ontario Book Publishing Tax Credit, and through Ontario Creates.

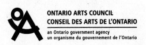

ONTARIO CREATES

ONTARIO ARTS COUNCIL
CONSEIL DES ARTS DE L'ONTARIO
an Ontario government agency
un organisme du gouvernement de l'Ontario

Canada Council   Conseil des arts
for the Arts   du Canada

Canada

PRINTED AND BOUND IN CANADA

PRINTING: MARQUIS   5   4   3   2   1

To Josh, Grace, and Avery

As you got older, you started asking about the rings tucked away in my drawer and the jerseys hidden in the closet. You've rolled your eyes at my quirks and wondered what your dad was thinking when I've struggled to show my emotions. It's my hope that the chapters of this book, glimpses of your dad's story, might give you some answers . . . it might also explain why I sit alone at your games.

CONTENTS

FOREWORD

first set eyes on Justin Davis when he was 16 years old, playing in Cambridge, Ontario. I was taking a break from coaching during the 1994–95 season, and I watched him play on a scouting trip at the Galt Gardens. He's one of those guys who you don't really notice until the game is over and you realize he's got a goal and a couple of assists. He was a good skater with really soft hands. Everything he does is quiet, and he played really well in his own end, which is why he fit in so well for me down the road. We didn't take him in the 1995 OHL Draft because it was rumoured that he was headed for the NCAA, and we didn't want to waste a pick. In his rookie year with the Kingston Frontenacs, it seemed like he scored against us every time we played each other. When he was playing with the Soo Greyhounds a couple of years later, he was really struggling. He didn't fit in with his coach's style of physical play, but I knew he would fit in perfectly in Ottawa. I called the Soo and said, "I'll take Justin Davis and I'll give you a draft pick or the waiver money, whatever you want." We ended up getting Justin for a sixth-round pick, and he became an unheralded scorer for us for two years and led the 1999 Memorial Cup in scoring. Justin's pass to Matt Zultek for the tournament-winning goal was one of the most important passes in 67's history. Adding Justin to our team was one of the best trades I ever made, and he was a huge part of the Ottawa 67's. I wish the very best for all of my former players, and I hope this book helps not only Justin, but also all of the parents out there dreaming of NHL success for their own kids. I'm glad that I had a part in Justin's career and that I was there when he needed a "coach" the most.

— BRIAN KILREA

INTRODUCTION

Y ou may have seen the cover of this book and asked yourself, *why?* Why would an "average" hockey player whose name barely registers with hockey fans write a book, and why would anyone bother to read it? Why would this player think that anyone would spend time reading his story when his entire hockey career is currently being overshadowed by his 16-year-old son? Well, it's complicated. The world of hockey has had a grand reawakening over the last couple of years, and to quote the legendary Canadian hockey broadcaster Bob Cole, "Everything is happening." Since 2020, a growing number of high-profile coaches have been fired because of past transgressions, and many more are secretly feeling the heat. I can guarantee you there are numerous behind-the-scenes apology tours happening as we speak, orchestrated by abusive coaches looking to maintain their place inside the game. But the dressing room doors have opened, and these predators can no longer hide behind their organizations. At the same time, junior hockey has had to address decades of hazing incidents, the research being done on CTE and repetitive brain injury has been eye-opening for former players, and Don Cherry's firing has the NHL distancing itself from its storied past. Add Akim Aliu's letter addressing the systemic racism in the game, and one thing is certainly clear: hockey needs to get better.

When Akim Aliu first told his story in 2020, my reaction was that he was soft and needed to toughen up. In my mind, he was a terrible team player and he sounded like an egotistical, cancerous presence. We all participated in the same initiations, we were all treated terribly by veteran players, and racism was just something that we normalized. I thought he was the issue; it was our job to conform to the norms of the hockey world. Varying from those norms, especially as a player of colour, was highly frowned upon. What's said in the room stays in the room, and it appeared to me that Akim was breaking the hockey code wherever he went. Then this memoir happened. I started to see myself through my son's eyes as a 16-year-old rookie all over again. Would I want him to have the same experiences in hockey? Akim had Tiger Balm put in his jock, his equipment thrown on the roof, he was bullied and tormented in front of his coach, asked to strip naked in a bus bathroom with the heat cranked up, cross-checked in the mouth at practice — losing seven teeth before being challenged to fight — called the N-word by a coach, and treated differently at every level because of the colour of his skin. In his letter, he remembered being told that he didn't get the "culture" of hockey. I now realize that we never understood the word culture. We used the word as an excuse, or an alibi, to carry out these hideous acts on minors that had been a tradition for decades. The difference for me was that I looked the same as everyone else. I soon realized that I was the issue, not Akim. Throughout my career, I was complicit in this behaviour, and I never stood up to stop it. I was ignorant. One of my coaches used to ask an Indigenous teammate if it would be easier to send him a smoke signal than explain the drill, and anyone with an Indigenous background would be called "Chief" or some other discriminatory slur.

I heard the N-word numerous times in the dressing room, in the stands, and on the ice, and although I knew it was wrong and wouldn't say it myself, in my mind it wasn't *my* problem. One of my childhood friends, while playing pro hockey in Germany, had bananas thrown at him during a game, but I never asked what I could do to help. Afraid of risking my own career by taking a stand, I never once spoke up to say this was wrong. It has taken me a long time to get to this place. When you are immersed in a world that tells you how to think, act, and behave from the time you are five years old, it's tough to see things differently. At some point, you need to step away from the game and see things from a distance. My friend Darren was recently explaining to one of our former teammates, Chris George, that he was treated differently in the OHL, and that he wasn't given the same opportunities that we were because he was Black. Chris should've been the coach's favourite player: he played physical, was highly skilled, and loved to fight. He was surprised at how we saw things. When a Black hockey player doesn't realize that he's being treated differently, and his path to the NHL looks much different from our journey, it's no surprise that it took me this long to see things through a different lens.

Chris, a teammate at Western, tells a story about walking down the street in London, Ontario, and being attacked by a biker. It started with racial slurs and he was knocked unconscious. The biker had brass knuckles on and he left Chris unconscious, lying limp on the sidewalk. He had to miss hockey because of a concussion and because he couldn't put his helmet on — he had that many stitches in his head. So what was his thought process after this incident? "I just remember thinking that I didn't want to get in trouble and get kicked off the team for being that Black guy who is causing trouble. It was a scenario that I look back at and think, how could I feel that guilt or concern?" It should have been different. If that was me being jumped on the street, we would have done everything to find the perpetrator and report the crime. For Chris, staying silent was what he felt he had to do to keep playing hockey. Nobody was charged, nothing was reported. The game of hockey continued and Chris stayed silent. Why did it take 20 years to realize that this was not right?

With the recent events surrounding Jordan Subban, Boko Imama, and Jalen Smereck, ignorance has once again reared its ugly head. All three players have endured racial taunting through various gestures or through the use of slurs. I can guarantee you that this isn't their first time dealing with these issues. Why are these incidents still happening, and what can we do to fix them? Well, for one, I grew up having just one Black teammate, and things haven't changed much since. From minor hockey to the NHL, Black players stand out, and players such as Jordan Subban have to grow up with thick skin, ready to respond to and defend themselves against verbal and physical acts of racism. I want to help ensure this is not the reality for the next generation of hockey players.

Only now do I have the courage to say that I was the one who was soft; although, it's easy to admit it in retrospect. I wasn't willing to risk my own career to stand up for others, and neither were my teammates. Players of colour fought through adversity every day just to have the same opportunities I did, and we were told this was okay and our coaches reinforced it, from minor hockey up to the NHL. Did I realize any of this before I sat down to collect my thoughts on my average career? Of course not, and that is why I am so disappointed in myself. I owe Akim Aliu and anyone one else who wasn't given an equal opportunity an apology.

Let me say the quiet part out loud: hockey is geared towards white, affluent athletes who can afford the extra training and coaching that comes with it. My son plays hockey. I know 15-year-old players who work with a nutritionist, a skills coach, a power skating coach, and a strength and conditioning coach, and who have the financial access to gain that extra edge. Registration for one year of rep hockey in Canada can cost upwards of $10,000, while a year of house league hockey can cost up to $600, not including the cost of skates and equipment. This is an expensive endeavour to find out if your son or daughter even enjoys the game. The sport is just too competitive and expensive for low-income families and at-risk communities, so the big question remains: How do we make the game accessible to everyone?

I have discussed this topic with multiple former players of colour, as I know my opinion and viewpoints mean nothing. I have never encountered the issues these players faced, and in order to gain an understanding of the topic, I know I must listen. But the conversations I have had have made me realize it's going to take time, money, and the acceptance of change from those within the game in order for hockey to be a game for everyone. True diversity means including everyone from a range of ethnic and social backgrounds, different genders and sexual orientations, and those with disabilities. It will not be until we regularly see these groups represented on the ice that these issues will be solved.

A great example of change is the recent hiring of Vancouver Canucks' assistant general manager, Émilie Castonguay. She played NCAA Division I hockey, has a bachelor's degree in finance, a law degree, interned for the Montreal Canadiens, speaks two languages, and has been a certified NHLPA agent for seven years. She can see hockey in a different light and has shown she is dedicated to improving the game. Hires like this is how we make hockey accessible for everyone. We must eliminate the archaic attitudes of the past to change the future. After all, hockey is a great game, and diversity will only make it better.

I'm proud to say that my friend and former teammate Chris George is now the head of the Hockey Diversity Alliance (HDA). I know he will succeed in the HDA's goal of creating policy and rule changes that will make the game more inclusive. I support the HDA's goal of growing hockey in communities that otherwise wouldn't have access to the sport, and I look forward to seeing grassroots programs for kids who represent the many different cultures that make our country great. Hopefully, this is just the beginning.

This is where I come in. Shortly after I retired, I reluctantly found myself immersed in the hockey world through coaching, mentorship, and skills training. Much like a member of an organized crime family, every time I tried to distance myself from the game, I would somehow get pulled back in. Parents, students, and players would always ask my opinion on hockey's current events because "you played professionally" and short answers would turn into long drawn-out conversations. The truth is, *I think I hate hockey*. I hated hockey at many points when I played, I hated it at the end of my career, and I think I hate it now. I despise how the game treated me at vulnerable times in my life, and I resent how it still affects parts of my life today. This is why things are complicated. Hockey is what made me the person I am today and is what gave me the short-lived fame that I never really wanted. I want to investigate why I loved hockey so much, so many years ago, and why I had a passion to play the game for most of my life. Maybe, by putting pen to paper, I can jog some small bits of my memory and find out when the fire inside me burned out. I need to find out what happened to the nine-year-old boy who would carry his bag a kilometre after school just to play shinny at the local arena. Why is this boy now an extremely jaded man, writing about the game he once loved, and how will this book help him heal?

While writing this book I had the opportunity to talk to countless former teammates and friends about their experiences in hockey. I kept waiting for them to tell me that what I was writing was incorrect, and that their experiences were more positive than mine. I wanted to use these conversations to help me uncover what I did wrong: Why do I feel the way I feel, and why am I in so much pain? But I quickly realized that we all quietly struggled with the same issues and that people I had known forever were only just becoming comfortable talking about their feelings. I was not alone. And if I was finally willing to share my feelings in a public space, then maybe my friends would be encouraged to do the same. I never wanted to be the emotional wet blanket at a social gathering, but I had become a listening ear for venting friends. In the initial stages of writing, teammates would specifically ask what I was writing about and it always led us down the same dark, twisted path. This is what I kept hearing:

"I had an Oxy addiction, and I combined it with alcohol. Eventually, I moved on to Morphine. Someone found me unconscious one day, and I realized I couldn't do this anymore. This had been going on since junior."

"I have been taking pills since Junior B. The team doctor prescribed me medi- cation to take away all of the anxiety I was feeling."

"Once I started seeing a therapist, I realized that what I was dealing with as an adult was a result of my hockey days. I can finally breathe and come to terms

with what I am feeling. Some days I get up at two in the afternoon, but my kids know those are my bad days."

The most common thing I heard, however, is the following:

"I realize now that I have always struggled with drugs and alcohol. I needed to be the 'fun' guy that everyone wanted me to be. The problem is, I wanted that person to stop. I started to avoid hanging out with my friends so I wouldn't become that person. It affected my marriage, my work, and all of my relationships. Only now do I recognize who I am after seeking help. I was in a dark place."

It has been exhausting to say the least. I spent over 20 years avoiding any real emotion, and I managed to block out anything to do with my feelings. I read posts on social media and listen to former players talk on the radio, and I can hear the effects that the game has had on them. They are not yet capable of seeing things clearly, but hopefully they will one day seek the help they need. I assume for many people, including some close friends, I am the foolish one. Protect the hockey code and keep your feelings buried, right? The problem is, the hockey world forgot about me a long time ago, so what am I protecting? It may take others a while before they see their own pain, and I will be there to help when they do. I can now say that I know myself better than I ever have before.

There are three other motives that are driving me to put my thoughts on paper. The first involves concussions and CTE. Those three simple letters, C-T-E, something I had never even heard of 10 years ago, are like a death sentence for me. I live in fear each day that my hands are shaking more than they used to, that my memory is fading, and that I won't remember things about myself that I want my kids to know. I see friends and former teammates struggling more and more, and I wonder if that will happen to me. People encourage me to see a doctor, but deep down, I'm terrified that my greatest fears will become a reality. Life is easier to live when you're in denial. I've had between 10 and 15 concussions over the course of my career. Two of those concussions were major, involving bleeding on the brain and a hospital stay. Five others were diagnosed, and I was treated with the proper care. The rest of them flew under the radar as a result of medical negligence or misinformation. Do you think concussion information was passed on with the player after a trade was made? Of course not. Concussions were treated and forgotten about or branded as a sign of toughness, both fueled by complete ignorance. Trade the player, trade the problem. Grade 1 concussions were considered minor bumps involving fuzzy moments that would be hidden from the team. It was our choice to play, and it allowed us to keep our place in the lineup. I'm not claiming to be special in any way, because if you ask any other player from my era, they experienced the exact same treatment. As science continues to evolve and we evaluate the research and evidence of continued brain trauma, the simple fact is, my past scares the crap out of me.

The second major reason for doing this is my family. I've always been an introvert and nobody knows much, if anything, about what I have experienced. I want my kids to know their dad, and I'm tired of hiding who I was, who I am, and what I am thinking today. I want to celebrate my hockey accomplishments, and, indirectly, I want to prepare my kids for my future. My moods are a roller coaster from day to day and there are times when I don't feel like myself. I need my kids to see what events shaped their father and why I am so protective of their future. I won't let people take advantage of them and impact their love of whatever they choose to do. I've learned from my own life, and it won't happen again. Most of all, I want my kids to read this book and know that their dad had an impact on the game of hockey. Am I afraid of what people will think, how my family will react, or how strangers will view me when I walk into an arena? Not a chance. This process feels therapeutic and may be more beneficial than seeing a doctor . . . for now. The game of hockey is broken, it leaves scars inside us we keep hidden, and only now am I ready to talk about it.

Lastly, I want to be able to shed some light on what is happening to the game. I was hazed, brutally, at three different levels. These acts should never be inflicted on anyone against their will. On the other hand, some of these traditions did lead to team bonding and eliminated entitlement. I want to investigate this negative hazing culture by looking at my own career and figuring out what the missteps were. The question is, what can we do to improve our positive hockey culture of inclusivity, accessibility, hard work and sacrifice without negatively impacting someone's mental health and their hockey career? Let's be clear, my opinions are my own and by no means perfect. My memory of events may not be the same as others' because we may have had a different way of seeing things. The people I mention by name have all been contacted, and I mention them because they had a positive impact on my career and my life. If I don't mention someone by name, it's because I don't want to affect their career if they are still inside the game. That's not the purpose of this book. Hopefully, they've changed and have adapted to the current times. Maybe one of them will read this and know that what they did was not right. After all, most of us were just kids living away from our families, trying to make our way in the complicated game of hockey. The adults were supposed to be the responsible ones in the room.

CHAPTER 1
REMEMBER, I'M SEVEN
(Minor Hockey Flamborough "A" and Halton "AAA")

I grew up in a sleepy little town called Carlisle. It was a small, affluent rural Ontario town, and my house was situated in a well-to-do subdivision 30 minutes from the closest movie theatre or mall. I had everything I needed, with close friends on my street, a swimming pool in the backyard, and a bike for all my transportation needs. I was a sports addict, and I spent every hour of each day outside playing sports. Wiffle ball in the backyard, road hockey in the driveway, and even the odd golf ball driven over the roofs of the houses nearby. I created uprights for kicking field goals in the backyard, a soccer net for shootouts, and I spent countless hours throwing a ball against a wall until I hit an eavestrough and had to hide from Dad.

My true passion was hockey. I could spend days playing road hockey with friends, until it was too cold to play outdoors and we had to move the game inside. I created a mini hockey arena in our basement, complete with the odd blood stain on the carpet. We spent hours curving plastic mini sticks over the stove and arguing about rule violations and disallowed goals. Baseball and soccer occupied my summers, but when they came to an end, I couldn't wait for the hockey season to begin.

I was an incredible minor hockey player. I really was. This is one of the few times you'll hear me brag. I played A hockey in Flamborough, and at the time, it was my NHL. While A hockey in the 1980s certainly wasn't the highest level of rep hockey, in a small town, it was everything. Most people nowadays think that the best hockey players play AAA hockey, and everything else is secondary. In reality, AAA hockey is just the highest level of hockey in areas with populations large enough to accommodate multiple levels, but some of the best players on these AAA teams come from the A teams in smaller communities. Our small-town parents in the 1980s had little interest in commuting over an hour for practice, so A level hockey was our only option. If I tried to explain this to a hockey parent now, they would think this was a mild form of child abuse.

Kids like me didn't really have their sights set on playing in the Ontario Hockey League or the NHL. We were just small-town kids playing organized hockey with the dream of an Ontario Minor Hockey Association (OMHA) Championship. It wasn't in our DNA to hate the Toronto Marlies or the Jr. Canadiens, as our rivals were from Hespeler, Preston, and other "concrete jungles." We knew deep down that our best players were just as good as those playing in AAA centres, but our overall team depth was not even close. Usually, small-town teams consisted of one superstar, two or three really good players, three average players, and five players who just filled out the roster. If the roster fillers could put their equipment on by themselves and could crossover in one direction, they were on the team. Skating backwards was a bonus, and these players would buy time for the superstar players to get water and rest up for their next shift. Last year, I was looking at some of my old tournament programs, and it was amazing to see the number of players from Atom A hockey teams who eventually went on to play in the OHL and the NHL.

In those days, your local hockey team transitioned to your baseball team when the season was over, and your friend's dad was usually the volunteer coach. His only qualifications seemed to be that he was from the town you lived in and he had ample time on his hands. The reality was that you only had seven or eight good athletes your own age in town anyway, so sports teams were always limited in their depth. We never thought of playing AAA hockey because it didn't exist in Carlisle, and who needed AAA when we got to play on a team with our best friends? Why would anyone want to play with kids they didn't even know? At the end of the day, playing with our friends was all that mattered. We didn't have individual skills coaches, power skating instructors, shooting coaches, or strength trainers. Our skills coach was our head coach, who could barely skate, power skating consisted of skating the circles because it forced you to turn in both directions, and strength training was riding your bike to practice with your bag on your shoulder.

My time in A level hockey can be summarized like this: scoring 200 goals a year and being hated for it. I don't mean that they disliked me — they actually hated me. Most of my own teammates' parents were jealous, the other teams' parents told their sons to hurt me, and my parents almost always sat alone. What most people never realized at the time was that I heard what they were saying and I understood what was happening around me. I was just a quiet kid, I liked to hang out with my family, I went to church, and I always treated people with respect. I never put myself ahead of the team, and I was very uncomfortable with my success and the drama it brought. It was common for me to score up to five goals a game, and I was becoming embarrassed about how good I was and how easy it came. I started exiting every game looking down at my boots as I walked through the arena lobby, choosing to bury my head and avoid eye contact with everyone. It was just easier to meet my parents in the car. *I was seven years old.*

I was still enjoying the game, but that negativity will be etched into my memory forever. I will never forget a playoff game in Woolwich, Ontario, when I was eight years old. Early in the second period, the other team's parents were taunting me, calling for my head in a non-contact game. I scored a goal late in the game to put us in the lead, and I skated to the corner to celebrate with my teammates. When I looked up from the scrum, there was an overweight 50-year-old woman screaming at me to "f*&# off" and pointing double middle fingers my way. Classy. On the way home, I asked my dad why that lady was so upset with me, but he struggled to come up with an explanation.

So why is all of this important? They say your childhood shapes who you are, and hockey taught me early on that people didn't seem to like me. I thought that maybe I was arrogant and that scoring three goals a game was selfish. After a while I decided that if I was on a breakaway and I had already scored in the game, I would just stop, curl inside the blue line, and wait for a teammate to join the rush so I could pass to him instead of trying to score myself. It looked ridiculous but it prevented parents from saying stupid things. When my dad finally asked the Flamborough Hockey Association (FHA) if I could play an age group up because I wasn't being challenged, they told him that nobody from Flamborough was ever going to amount to anything, so go back and play at your own level. The board members were upset at him for even asking, and they made sure that their message was loud and clear. Trust me, I never forgot it, and it was what drove me to my hockey success.

Things didn't seem to get any better the following season. After all of these years, I can still remember an Atom tournament in Mississauga, Ontario, over the Christmas holidays. I scored six goals in the championship game, and our team won the championship. At the trophy presentation, the organizing committee awarded the MVP trophy to another player on my team who had scored a goal late in the 7–1 win. I remember taking my helmet off, putting my head down, and starting the skate to the PA announcer to accept the MVP award when I stopped quickly in my tracks. I was embarrassed. My dad secretly walked into the organizing room after the game and asked the convenor why they had given the award to another player. He wasn't looking for the MVP recognition, as my dad was a humble man, but he was looking for an explanation to tell his eight-year-old son on the way home. The convenor said that I probably won awards all the time and that other kids need to win awards at some point, too. I spent the drive home in tears, looking out the window and wondering what I was doing wrong. Would it be easier if I just stopped scoring goals and tried to blend in? Most eight-year-olds don't understand resentment, and this has had a huge effect on who I am today. I was never able to properly celebrate achievements, and I continue to feel shame with any acknowledgement or accolade that I receive. Whenever I won an MVP award or a trophy, I always hid it in my pocket or hockey bag for the walk through the arena lobby. I envied the other kids coming out of the dressing room with their awards around their necks, smiling with pride. I just wanted to fit in with everyone else.

None of this is meant to come across as whining. I was a fortunate kid who had a nice house, lived in a great neighbourhood, was gifted at sports, and had the opportunity to play the game I loved. So far, much of what I've written might come across as a first world humblebrag. *My life was terrible because I scored too many goals and people were mean to me.* But the point of writing this book is to figure out why I stopped loving the game and learn why I have so much emotional baggage. When I started to reflect on this period and collect my thoughts, everything came rushing back. Embarrassment, resentment, adult jealousy, and self-esteem issues flooded over me like a tidal wave. I can remember these incidents like they happened yesterday, yet I can't remember my kids' birthdays and what I had for breakfast this morning. These incidents have obviously had a deep impact on my life, and it wasn't until I began writing that I ever thought about my past. It's funny how you can block out the clouds of your history when you focus on the sunshine and roses.

Things hit their tipping point when I turned 11. We had just one sports store within a 20-minute radius of Carlisle. It was called Gym Dandee, and if you needed something in a hurry, this wasn't the store for you. The owners, a married couple, made it their job to smoke as many cigarettes as possible inside the small space, in the shortest amount of time. It was a smell you never forgot. The people who ran the place were on the board of the FHA, and they were influential people in the small world of Flamborough Hockey. To get a sense of their character and qualifications for the job, you have to hear only one story. One day at the Carlisle Arena, my friend Scott, who was eight at the time, was arguing with the husband. In a fit of rage, the adult FHA board member hung the poor kid by his jacket on a hook in the dressing room, closed the door, and left him there to fend for himself. Perfect role model for a youth sports organization. Apparently, my dad had ruffled some board members' feathers the previous year, when he applied to move me up an age group. The dream team couple was not happy about it and shifted their focus from smoking in their shop to waging a personal vendetta against me. So how do you deal with a ten-year-old in your organization who you now have a grudge against? Well, that's pretty simple . . . they assigned their two sons to ref my home games at the Carlisle Arena. Whenever I did anything borderline on the ice, their boys would give me a penalty and would mock me on the way to the penalty box, trying to incite me into another penalty. If I asked for an explanation of why I was in the box, I would receive another penalty or a 10-minute misconduct. It was embarrassing for me, but that seemed to be the way my life was going.

I've had the pleasure of instructing at an adult hockey camp in St. Catharines for the last six years. People always raise an eyebrow when I tell them that these "campers" are actually adults between the ages of 30 and 65, signing up for a stayover hockey camp in a hot dorm in the middle of July. The reason I keep coming back year after year is that these campers remind me of the love I felt for hockey when I started playing and what it looks like to be passionate about lacing up your skates. These adults come to camp wanting to learn basic skills and they can't wait to get on the ice each and every day. They skate for four hours each afternoon and are put together with medical tape, tensor bandages, and an athletic therapist, but they show up for each session ready for more. This is what hockey felt like when I was much younger and why I wanted to play the game in the first place. This is what hockey should feel like now. At camp there are no angry parents banging on the glass, no hockey association politics, and no long car rides home with a disgruntled dad. But you will find a huge smile on a 50-year-old man's face after he learns to stop on his weak side and see the pure joy of a 45-year-old woman who has just raised the puck for the first time. This should've been the joy I felt, but at the ripe old age of nine, that was long gone.

I was recently listening to a podcast on the way to work, and the hosts were talking about a survey pertaining to what kids remembered the most about their youth sports experience. The number one thing that kids reported having negative memories about? The car ride home.

That's not surprising at all. What were the positive things that these same kids remembered? Seeing their grandparents in the crowd or stopping for food on the way home. Seems like a pretty simple analysis of our behaviour, doesn't it? I decided five years ago to never talk about a practice or game with my kids in the car, even if it killed me. Trust me, there have been some long, silent rides home. My dad was the same way. Most of our rides involved sports radio, discussions about world issues, or just silence. The only thing that would ever initiate a car ride conversation with my own kids now is a severe lack of effort or bad body language. That's it. Everything else can wait. Most of the time, something will come up a week later, but I'll shape it as a positive, with a focus on how to work on fixing their mistakes. You forgot to pick up a trailer on a 3-on-2? You never shot the puck on a 2-on-1? You stopped moving your feet in the second period? A week later on the way to the game, I may say, "Try shooting today if you get a two-on-one; you have a great shot." It hasn't been easy, but it has made the car rides home more enjoyable for everyone, and it has led to some great conversations about things that actually matter. Sports is about relationships, and the time in the car is the most valuable parenting time I have. Do you think my daughters would ever say, "Dad, can we just drive around for three hours today and talk?" So if we can make the car ride a safe place and get grandma and grandpa out to more games, maybe sports can actually be fun . . .

Fortunately, my time in Flamborough minor hockey was coming to an end. As an act of good fortune, the Halton Hurricane AAA team was created in 1991. Halton allowed players from Milton, Georgetown, Orangeville, Hillsburgh, Erin, and, most importantly, Flamborough to have access to the highest level of hockey in Ontario. I made the team in Pee Wee, and it was one of the best things that ever happened to my career. It didn't take long for me to realize that I could keep up with the top players in my age group and that hockey could actually be fun. Playing in Halton allowed me to make some friends that I have to this day, and we continue to run into each other as our own kids begin their journey in the game. I needed to leave my comfort zone in Flamborough to realize my potential. Years later, when I was asked to play in top prospect tournaments across Ontario, I realized that someone from Flamborough *could* actually do something special in hockey. I had to work extremely hard, but I always had the drive to compete. Hockey became my passion, and I was ready for the future.

There was a major difference between A and AAA hockey. Parents may not think so, but the game is much different. The speed increases, the players are bigger, and it continues all the way up the hockey ladder. My first OHL training camp felt like it was in fast forward, and my first taste of the NHL felt like warp speed. In the hockey world, there is an ongoing joke that as you age, your former career improves. For example, if you played AA hockey when you were younger, you tell people that you could've played AAA but the coach was an idiot or your dad didn't want to drive that far. If you actually played Junior B hockey, by the time you're 40 years old, you actually played in the OHL. People would cover their lies by saying that they didn't make it any further because they got injured or the coach didn't like them. Remember, this was long before you could be fact checked on a phone or laptop. If you actually played in the OHL, there was always a reason why you never made it to the next level, and most likely, your agent screwed you. It was a common occurrence, and the arrival of hockeyDB and Elite Prospects have given hockey players ammunition to combat this behaviour and it has provided some good laughs along the way. I remember being at a party one summer, listening to a person go on about how they played for the Ottawa 67's and telling anyone who would listen that they were going back for the upcoming season. He had no idea that an actual player from the team was sitting right beside him, but it was enjoyable to just listen to the lies. It still happens in men's league change rooms across the country. Parents are dying to have their children play the highest level of hockey, and they love to change their own hockey resumés along the way.

I've read a ton of literature about parents devoting their entire lives to the advancement of their kids' *supposed* dreams. But whose dream is it really? Many of these cases involve parents who have never even played a high-level sport and are trying to live vicariously through their own children. I call it "A" Hockey Syndrome. As in, the dad only ever played house league or A level hockey, but in their mind if their own parents had put more time into their development or if the AA coach hadn't screwed them, they would have made the NHL. They won't let the same thing happen to their own kid, and they will put every resource possible into making this dream a reality. When I coached AAA hockey, I always made sure to have one mandatory parent/child scrimmage a year to evaluate the on-ice talent of my most vocal critics. How can you claim I'm teaching the defence-men incorrectly when you can't even skate backwards? These parents are seeking gratification through their kid's potential success, throwing away well-earned money and their kid's childhood in the process. Someone once told me that if you want something more than your own kid or the athletes you coach, then something is seriously wrong.

When I talk to former pro athletes, it's always refreshing to hear the perspective that less is more. The idea of overscheduling a youth athlete does not guarantee future stardom. If my son or daughter wants to take extra skills sessions, I will sign them up. If they want to play hockey in the spring or soccer in the winter, I'll sign them up. I will only empower them to put in the work that they want to put in. I can't want something for my kids if they don't have the passion for it. My son has avoided spring hockey for years, and he has never had the urge to attend morning power skating sessions. I have always been fine with that. Last year, he started asking me workout questions and wanted to do some on-ice skills sessions to work on his shooting and footwork. I finally signed him up because he actually wanted it. My favourite quote on our dressing room wall in junior was, "Nothing great was ever achieved without enthusiasm." Is there a more relevant quote to describe young athletes' development?

It's frightening how obsessed hockey parents have become and how often the wrong people are in positions of power. It always seems like the people in control have ideals that are the furthest away from reality. Some parents would do anything to change that AA to AAA on their kid's jacket. When I was moving up the minor hockey ladder, jealousy created some pretty spiteful parents. People forget about the damage this can do to a kid. Do they ever take the time to think that their spitefulness towards another player on the team may affect their own relationship with their child? Living your NHL fantasy through your son is a dangerous endeavour. For players with a truthful, hard-earned resumé, the amount of sacrifice involved and the pain that comes with it becomes a sense of pride. For someone to say they accomplished something when they never came close is offensive. I thought of this with the feel-good story of David Ayres, the zamboni driver/practice goalie, and the Toronto Maple Leafs. Most hockey fans would say that it's a great story, and deep down they believe that could have been them if they just got their big break. Who you don't hear about are the numerous goalies who put in years of sacrific but never fulfilled their NHL dream, who were extremely jealous of the attention Ayres was getting. Their envy comes from years of riding buses in the minors, moving their families, ACL surgery, hip surgery, and the mental fatigue of it all. That's the pain of being a hockey player who comes extremely close to their dream but just doesn't have enough to make it.

I'm the complete opposite of this type of person. I live in fear that people will find out that I wasn't that good. I don't like discussing hockey with strangers out of fear that someone may have talked to a former teammate and was told that I was soft, that I couldn't skate, and that I hated to fight. I actually won a Memorial Cup and was the leading scorer in the tournament. I won a university championship, and I am still the all-time points leader at the University of Western. I was drafted 85th overall by the Washington Capitals in 1996. It's a resumé that most people would be extremely proud of. Where I should feel pride in my accomplishments, I feel embarrassment. Deep down, I wonder if I deserve half of the success that I attained. So when I think about this anxiety that I feel, I think about the eight-year-old boy walking out of the arena with his head down and the impact this has had on him. This pain is what makes me want to write, and I want people to know about my experiences. I want coaches to think about the effect they have on a child when they are screaming at a player in novice. I want parents to think about the impact they have when they stir up jealousy over a player being better than their son. Most of all, I want hockey families to enjoy their time together and to realize this is just a game and not a journey to fame.

Not all of my memories are tough to swallow. Hockey can be a fun sport and have a positive impact on young players. I remember going to Mother's Pizza on road trips with my team, collecting pins from my opponents to put on my jacket, singing war chants in the hallways on our way to the ice, and the excitement of getting to play a game. I remember rushing off the school bus every day and throwing my bag into the ditch so I could get the road hockey pads on and pretend to be Grant Fuhr. I remember the excitement of having a bright white Titan hockey stick that never broke or got frayed, but got thinner and more dangerous the more you played. I smile when I think of the road hockey sticks that we used. If we had sticks like this now, parents would have their kids wearing eye goggles and neck guards to play on the street. I remember the joy of a snow day and going to my neighbour's house to play *NHL* on his Sega Genesis for eight straight hours. We would eat as many Pizza Pops and Eggo waffles a kid could stomach. I remember travelling to tournaments and riding in the back of my friend's station wagon, facing the opposite direction and staring at cars behind us for hours on end. We felt like we were in another world, separated from our parents. It's funny that these memories were all exclusive of adults and the people who actually ruin the game. Hockey was a competition, hockey was friendship, hockey was riding in the car with my dad, and, more importantly, hockey was sometimes enjoyable.

CHAPTER 2
A BOY IN A MAN'S WORLD
(Flamborough Gamblers — Junior C)

After playing AAA in Halton for a handful of years, I was invited to try out for the Junior B Milton Merchants. It was an exciting opportunity, but I was extremely nervous. Unfortunately, the nerves were for nothing: I was cut after the very first skate. Not only was I cut, I was also humiliated. On a sheet of paper posted in the lobby of the Thompson Arena, my name, along with three others, was written in big black marker, letting me (and the rest of the world) know I would not be advancing to the next skate. Even better, my name was spelled Justin Davies. It doesn't take long for the hockey world to humble you, and it was the first time in my life that I was cut from anything. It was an embarassing experience, but it motivated me to prove the evaluators wrong. Hockey had always been easy and now, for the first time, someone had said that I wasn't good enough.

A short time after getting cut in Milton, I was invited to try out for the local Junior C team, the Flamborough Gamblers. The Gamblers played out of the old North Wentworth Arena on Highway 6, and it was only a 15-minute drive from my house. I attended a couple of skates during the tryout period, and I eventually made the team. So what does a 15-year-old earn while playing Junior C hockey in his hometown? I negotiated $25 a week for gas, even though I couldn't drive, free Koho sticks, a pair of Bauer Supreme skates, and free equipment to be returned to the team at the end of the year. I was fresh into Grade 10, so the decision was easy. I told my parents I wanted to sign the contract immediately, before they took anything away. I was so naive at the time I didn't understand that the deal was basically under the table and the actual contract I was signing was a basic OHA waiver. The Gamblers took a school bus to all of their road games, but it felt luxurious to me. We had a trainer, a statistician, free tape, and I could keep all of my equipment at the rink. We even had a dedicated goal judge who once peed his pants in a double overtime game rather than leave his post behind the net. I thought I had won the lottery, and I couldn't wait to start.

Our coach that year was "Swervin" Ervin Hillebrand, and he was a beauty. Some of my teammates were as old as 21, and Erv coached everyone the same way: extremely hard. He liked to get angry and he loved to swear. Erv did a lot of yelling, but he was a good man with my best interests in mind, and he always made me laugh. I was no longer treated with kid gloves, and Erv knew hockey; it was a great place for me to play the season. I was very lucky. Erv would come into our dressing room and repeat the same thing before each game. "Battle zones, boys, battle zones. If you win the two feet on each side of the blue line, you will win the game. I lost a Junior C Championship five years ago because a player refused to get the puck out of this two-foot area. Win the blue line, win the game." I will never forget the words "battle zones" for as long as I live, but that was his ultimate goal. I hate to say it but the more I coach hockey, the more I realize Erv was right.

Practices were great, but they were very late at night. Monday nights were 9 p.m. to 10:30 p.m. and Wednesday nights were 9:00 p.m. to 11:00 p.m.

Most of the players on the team had jobs and they couldn't practice any earlier, but I was in Grade 10 with no care in the world. I always carpooled with my two buddies who lived on my street, and the highlight of the night was our Tim Hortons stop after practice. You may be wondering how a 42-year-old man can remember the time of his hockey practices 27 years ago. Well, this was when Tim Hortons had an actual baker, and not a 16-year-old kid who uses only a microwave or a toaster oven. Each night at 11:30 p.m., the baker would walk out of the kitchen, covered in flour, and carrying a tray of freshly baked donuts. I can still vividly see and smell the donuts to this day. Hot apple fritters, sugar twists, honey crullers, and a cold iced tea from the old fountain machine that sprayed iced tea everywhere. Life was simple, but life was good.

Every Monday morning at high school, I would gather my buddies at first break and share stories about the previous weekend's road trip and the bus ride conversations with the team. I was getting an advanced education in life, to say the least. I would always sit five rows ahead of the older guys, but close enough to hear everything that was being said. When conversations would wrap up, I would put on my Sony Walkman and listen to my newest mixtape, Ace of Base, or Jon Bon Jovi. From these bus trips, I learned how to cheat in school and how to play euchre, got a crash course in sex ed, and I knew not to speak unless I was spoken to. That was the golden rule of the bus, know your place and respect the veterans. We had a couple of 21-year-olds who treated me great and a bunch of 18- and 19-year-olds who made me feel like their little brother. I was a year removed from Grade 9, and looking back on it now, I was as naive as they come.

Early on in the season, I learned about a terrible ailment called the "Chippewa Flu." Apparently, this flu mostly affected veteran players. I arrived early for the team's third road trip of the year. You quickly learn that being on time for a bus is arriving 15 minutes earlier than the actual planned departure. I packed my hockey bag and stuffed it under the bus, found my seat near the front, and waited for the others to arrive. I remember thinking, *There are a lot of guys late today, there must be some serious traffic on the QEW.* Fifteen minutes later, we departed with only 12 players and two goalies. When I asked the trainer where everyone was, I was told that they have the Chippewa Flu. It was then explained to me that Chippewa was one of the toughest teams in the league, and they had a very small arena. So some guys would just call in sick to avoid playing the game. I didn't know this was an option, but I wish someone had told me about it. I integrated quickly into Junior C hockey that night, double shifting in a tiny rink in Chippewa, Ontario.

In my Junior C year, I stood six foot four and 140 pounds soaking wet with equipment on. I played the entire season in fear, as it was a men's league and I was still a boy deep down. To keep it simple for you, the league could get stupid. The Dundas Blues had a former OHL heavyweight who was already 21 years old and was like the boogeyman. Guys talked about him in the dressing room much like in the movie *Slap Shot*, and I knew never to hit him or make eye contact. If I stole the puck from him, I needed to skate away quickly and avoid the retaliation. Midway through the season, we had a home game against Dundas. During the pregame meeting, a new player who nobody had ever seen before walked into our dressing room. He introduced himself to the team and silently got dressed. I asked the guy next to me if we had made a trade and he said, "No, he's just here to fight tonight and he'll be gone by tomorrow." Sure enough, our new John Doe fought the other team's heavyweight twice that night and he was never seen again. He was our team's Keyser Söze and he was brought in to protect our home ice and, more importantly, guys like me.

In early October, the plans for the rookie party were put into place. I knew that the party was inevitable, but I really wasn't that nervous. How bad could it be, right? I saw the party as a rite of passage and a way to fit in with the older guys. I was still pretty naive, and this was the start of my indoctrination. We were told to arrive at the old Breezy Corners Motel on the corner of Highway 5 and Highway 6. Players had booked two rooms for a total value of $30 per room (bed bugs included), and they obviously spared no expense. It was a one-star hotel, and it would've been completely shut down if Tripadvisor had been in existence at this time. I think the only people using the hotel daily were truckers and escort services.

I showed up at 7 p.m. sharp and got in line to have my head shaved. We were told to shave our entire body beforehand or risk having it shaved by the team. I did what I was told as always, and I arrived with a body full of razor burn. The veterans proceeded to shave a Michigan Wolverines helmet into my head, and I was now through stage one of the initiation process. As mentioned, I was extremely tall and skinny, so without body hair and sporting a butchered haircut, I was not an attractive option for the opposite sex. Stage two involved us stripping down to our jocks and nothing else. We were loaded into a car bound for the local IGA in Waterdown. Upon arrival, I was told that I needed to go into the IGA and return with two cases of pop for mix at the party. Waterdown was not a big town back then, so I'm sure out of the 70 people who were in the IGA store that night, I knew 50 of them personally. I'll never forget standing in line with my bare butt showing and a jock covering my precious parts. My hair was looking like a complete disaster, and I was waiting, holding two cases of pop, embarrassed like a complete idiot. I calmly asked the cashier how her night was going, purchased the pop, and exited the store. We headed back to the motel and got ready for the rest of the night.

Stage three was where things got ugly. Three of the older veterans sat alone in one room, while the rest of the team drank excessively in the other. When I was called to the initiation room, I had to take off all of my clothes and enter the bathroom. On the floor was a cup of beer that I was told to drink. After drinking the beer, it was refilled and I was told to do five pushups with my genatalia landing in the cup with each rep. If I missed the cup, I had to do another pushup correctly. I realized very quickly that the previous rookie called into the initiation room did pushups into the the cup I just drank from. Of course in my simple, naive mind, I was worried about banging out five pushups, as I was not gifted in the pectoral region yet. When I returned to the first room, everyone was laughing at me and I started to drink heavily to forget what just happened. This was the night that I had my first beer, at 15 years old, in a rundown motel, completely naked with my teammates.

Nudity seemed to be a fixation for initiations at this time and these abnormal acts were made to seem routine. When I came out of the bathroom, the veterans celebrated me and made me feel like a hero and a "good rookie." In hindsight, the veterans were very good to me after this because I was playing well, I kept my mouth shut, and I made them laugh when I was allowed to speak. I followed the rules, but not everyone did. Some players were treated much worse than I was, but there was nothing I could do. I guess I was lucky to be shaved from head to toe and be forced to enter the IGA naked, in front of my community? I guess I was lucky to drink beer from a cup that someone else's genitals were in two minutes earlier and that I had to chase it down with my first 10 beers at the Breezy Corners Motel? I was 15 years old and I have no idea where I stayed that night. At the end of the party, I do remember watching Joe Carter's World Series–winning home run and running around the outside of the hotel, celebrating without any clothes on. My story of where I was when the Jays won the '93 World Series is much different than most of my friends. That was the beginning of my hockey indoctrination.

As the season was coming to a close, I was getting more comfortable with the style of play. The jump from Bantam AAA to Junior C was enormous. When I walked in the dressing room on a Friday night late in the season, I noticed our team was unusually excited. It turned out my teammates were planning to start a warm-up brawl in that night's game. At that time in junior hockey, referees never went onto the ice to supervise warm-up. You were lucky if the refs even peeked their heads out of their dressing room to see how much time was left on the clock. The plan for the brawl was for one of our older guys to fire a slapshot into the visitors end and to hit someone in the back with the puck. This would eventually start organized chaos and everyone would get to fight whoever they wanted. I was terrified. Bigger players never ended up with 140 pound 15-year-olds. That would be wishful thinking. I explained to the guys that this probably wasn't a good idea and we should try to win the game, as we were currently in fourth place. This was a big game in the standings and we shouldn't risk getting guys suspended. Out of the corner of the room I heard a veteran player say, "Hey, rookie, shut up!" I never said another word about it. I quickly grabbed the pregame notes and tried to pick out another guy my size and weight on the other team. It would be a bonus if he had really low penalty minutes as well. After extensive research, I eventually found my guy. Warm-up started and I couldn't focus on anything. I'm not sure if I even touched a puck during the first five minutes. I located my chosen fighting partner at the other end of the rink and zoned in on him. I mirrored his movements to make sure I stayed close to him at all times. Out of the corner of my eye, I watched a puck get hammered down the ice and hit the end glass, avoiding all of the players on the other team. Nothing happened. Two minutes later, another rocket was launched down the ice and it buckled an opposing player right in the spine. Time stood still. Players rushed to the red line and there was a lot of arguing, finger pointing, and pushing. I silently sidled up to my guy and made sure to get behind him so I could give him a gutless sucker punch and jump on his back, rendering him useless when the time came. I had a plan after all. Players squared off, punches were thrown, and before a giant melee could ensue, the refs came flying out of their dressing room half-dressed. Coaches managed to settle things down, and I lived to see another day. Finally, I could breathe once again. I hated this part of hockey, but looking back on it now, I do find some humour in it all. It's probably because I came out of it all in one piece.

When you remove some of the stupidity involved, Junior C was actually great hockey. We had pretty good fans, I played on a skilled line, and the promotions throughout the season were hilarious. One of the highlights that season was the KFC chicken race. During each home game, two fans got to choose one player each from our team to race from the blue line to the goal line during the first intermission. The fan who chose the winning player of the race received a free bucket of chicken from the Waterdown KFC, and the winning skater won a bucket of chicken as well. It was so ridiculous to come in from a period, losing 3–1, and have Erv scream at the team for being brutal, only to be interrupted by a volunteer who would peek their head in and say, "Davis, you got chosen for the chicken race, lace 'em up." It kept hockey in perspective because as soon as you thought the game was life or death, you were humbled by having to race for $10 worth of KFC. I ended up with four buckets of chicken that year. Junior C was always a little bit different, but it was an experience that I will never forget.

At the end of the day, I had a blast. I scored 40 goals and had 40 assists and made the league All-Star game. Locals would come out to watch the team play, fans were packed into most road arenas, and, best of all, it was free for me to play. Every time I broke a Koho, I got a brand new one, and I could tape my stick as many times as I wanted to. That never happened in AAA hockey — I was living large. I can still smell the mustiness of the dressing room in Flamborough, and I can still feel the bitter cold of walking into the room at 12 a.m. after a road game in February. Whenever I dropped my bag off in the dressing room after a road trip and went home free and easy, I felt like this was my little NHL. Little did I know that this was just the beginning of my career. The eight-year-old boy with dreams of an OMHA Championship was now dreaming of something much bigger. I was still scared most nights, but I tried not to show it. I was never afraid to go into the corner or the tough areas of the ice, but I never initiated contact and made sure not to upset anyone. I got my first penalty halfway through the year, and the entire bench stood up and clapped. It was embarrassing, but I deserved it. In the following years, I never consistently played with much grit or toughness, and I often wondered if that fear I felt in Junior C, along with not playing with my own age group, made me adapt to a different style. I had to constantly adjust to my surroundings, and if I stirred up any trouble, I had to answer the bell. This is much different than what kids experience today. Maybe I was just soft, and I was just a nice kid brought up in a good family. Either way, it was a memorable year and it was a decision that I'll never regret.

At the end of the season, I received numerous calls from OHL teams letting me know I was going to get selected in the upcoming draft. I had multiple phone interviews with teams, and I even received the high-end three-dollar VHS promotional tape from the league. The funny part is that I had never been to an OHL game, and I wasn't really sure what the league even was. There wasn't an OHL Network at the time, and the only OHL information for a kid from Carlisle was in *The Hockey News*, which I never read.

The Guelph Storms' arena was 25 minutes away from my hometown, but why would I watch an OHL game when *Hockey Night in Canada* was on TV in my family room. At that time, any underage players who were eligible (16 years old) had to go in the first three rounds of the OHL Draft or they could not be selected until the next year's draft. Two weeks before the draft, I received a phone call from a Sudbury scout who told me they were taking me in the third round and to make sure that I attended the draft in person. I couldn't have been happier or more excited.

My dad and I hopped in the car and drove to the 1994 OHL Draft in Belleville. We walked in, and I immediately regretted my decision to wear jeans and a t-shirt. Apparently, this draft thing was a big deal and every other kid was in a suit. I was without an agent at this time, so I sat in the crowd and tried to figure out this foreign process. I was having a little anxiety thinking about walking down to the draft floor in a pair of Request jeans and a Vuarnet t-shirt, but it was overshadowed by the excitement of eventually getting selected. My dad and I watched pick after pick until the end of the third round. When the third round finished and I still wasn't chosen, we were a little confused. We went over the list of players drafted once again, just in case we happened to miss my name. My dad had to ask a stranger nearby about the rules of the draft to make sure that I wasn't going to be picked later on, so we could leave without missing anything. The experience turned out to be another bump in the road and an opportunity to see that this game was going to be tough to navigate. Why would someone tell me I was going to be picked and that I should come to the draft? Did they accidentally forget about me on their draft list? I never heard from that scout again, but Sudbury was now on my list of hockey offenders, along with my Flamborough minor hockey friends, and the Milton Merchant coaching staff. I can understand why the OHL changed the format to an online draft many years later. It was a great decision that prevents embarrassment for the hundreds of players who tune in to the draft without hearing their name. My dad and I walked out to the parking lot and headed home. We grabbed some Wendy's at the first rest stop and tried to figure out what exactly had just happened as we travelled back to Carlisle.

CHAPTER 3
THE POTATO FARMER
(Cambridge — Junior B)

Over the summer, I had time to reflect on what I needed to do to get better. I worked out in my basement, using free weights and an old bench press, and I worked on my cardio by jogging or roller-blading around town. After the draft, I realized that having an agent was a good idea, so I signed an agreement with my first agent, Don Reynolds. He received an offer for me to play with the Caledon Canadiens in the Tier II Junior A loop for the upcoming season. They had money to burn and had had an amazing team the year before, with Bates Battaglia getting selected in the NHL Draft, but eventually lost in the league final. I met with Coach Greg Ireland, was assigned a billet family, and registered at the local high school. After the first couple of skates in August, my mom and I met with the coach once again, and he said that the team was going to move in a different direction. I must make a pretty good impression the first time people see me play hockey, as this was the second time in two years that I had been cut early on in the tryouts. This time I had been guaranteed a spot beforehand, so I must have made an extra special impression.

In another state of confusion, this time with my mom, we drove home and I tried to figure out my next steps. I have spent a lot of time over the years in the car contemplating my future, and it's a big reason why I still prefer silence in the car to this day. My agent called when I got home and said, "I'll pick you up tomorrow afternoon and we'll go meet with the coach in Cambridge. He's a potato farmer named Spud and I really think you'll like him. It's close to home and they have a pretty good team."

Don picked me up the next day in his Lexus, and we headed to Cambridge. I met with Spud for the first time and, fortunately, our paths have continued to cross in the hockey world over the years. Spud played a huge part in my career, and I consider him a friend to this day. He's an honest man, with a great sense of humour, and he was just what I needed at that time. Spud signed me after my first skate in Cambridge, and he was happy to have me on the team. Sometimes, it's just nice to be wanted, and it was a feeling I would experience throughout my hockey career. Cambridge actually worked out much better for me, as I could still live at home, and the drive was only 20 minutes away. I essentially received the same deal as the year before: sticks, skates, and team equipment. I did negotiate a slight pay increase to $50 a week for gas. This was a significant raise for a 16-year-old, and it was a brand new start to my career. I was driving a 1984 Ford Tempo named Gloria, with a Rene Russo poster pinned on the interior roof. I made enough mix tapes for the commute to last me the season, and I now had just enough money to spread my wings.

We played in the old Galt Arena Gardens that still stands today. It was a great junior rink, complete with a giant picture of Queen Elizabeth on one end of the arena. Our dressing room was an upgrade from Flamborough, but the walkway to get to the ice was built for a small child. I remember getting fired up for a game and then essentially having to crawl out of the tunnel to get to the ice. It was pretty funny to watch a whole junior hockey team do this in unison before each game. The league was extremely fast and it was great hockey. It was more my style, with it being an offensive game with less stupidity. There were teams in Elmira, Stratford, Listowel, Kitchener, Waterloo, Brantford, and Ohsweken. The majority of arenas were packed because it was the thing to do in town on a Friday night, and there were some great atmospheres to play in. Stratford had two NHL Draft picks, two players who would go on to the NHL, and two others who would play in the NCAA the following season. They were an awesome team, and in the middle of their league dynasty. More importantly, I learned some traditions continue on from Junior C to the Junior B level.

I arrived at the arena 15 minutes early for our first road game of the season to Ohsweken. Much like my time in Flamborough the year before, I hated to be late. I packed my hockey bag and grabbed my seat on the bus. We took a coach bus on the longer road trips in Junior B, and that was a novelty. After sitting for a couple of minutes, I asked another player, "Where is everyone?" The guy behind me muttered, "Bad case of the Ohsweken flu going around." Apparently, this disease affects players at each level of hockey. Ohsweken wasn't a great team, but they had a lot of veteran players, and the trip to the reserve wasn't for everyone. They had the best arena french fries in the league, though, and the pregame and postgame french fry line was a 15-minute wait. We won my first game in Ohsweken, and I had a couple of points. More importantly, I escaped injury free. I boarded the bus with my fries, took a deep breath, and said, "That wasn't too bad." Our assistant coach turned around, laughed, and said, "Yeah, I guess, if you like driving a bus home on the rims." I looked out the window and saw our bus driver staring at the tires as he was trying to figure out how to get air in them once again. We sat on the bus for three hours before the bus company arrived with two new tires and a compressor to fill the other two. Ohsweken 1 – Cambridge 0.

It was a pretty uneventful year and everything ran smoothly. Hockey was going well and we had a great dressing room. We must've listened to the *Reservoir Dogs* soundtrack every day, and I can still sing that album start to finish. I received my first fan letter and photo early in the season, from a girl in a local high school. She seemed attractive and started coming to some of our practices and games. When the second letter came a couple weeks later with some blood dripped on it, I thought it was best to cut off communication and find a new way out of the rink after practice. On the bright side, I finally had a fan.

Halfway through the season, talk of a rookie party came up again. I was now a veteran of the rookie party scene, and talk of another one didn't bother me or make me nervous. We had a great veteran group on the team and they respected everyone. Our captain, 20-year-old Glen Hopkins ("Hoppy"), had been on the team since he was 16 years old and was one of the nicest people I have ever met in hockey, and he always looked out for me. The party was held at a house in Cambridge, and it was uneventful. There was drinking, as always, and some girls in attendance, but nothing degrading or anything I'd later regret happened. That's the thing I learned in hockey, if you have a good captain and great leadership, the team seems to follow. This is reflected in how the rookies on the team are treated. Occasionally, players who were mistreated in their rookie season sought out retribution on the new class. A good leadership group can take control of this situation The party was a lot of fun and Hoppy brought me back to his place, making sure I got home safely.

Spud was the best thing that happened to me in Cambridge. He taught me how to be a professional and brought out the fun side of the game. I remember walking into his office one night after a game and Brian Kilrea was sitting there smoking a cigar and enjoying a cold beverage with Spud. Little did I know the impact that those two men would have on my life. Likewise, how many times I would see them enjoying a cold beer. Spud would spend time in the dressing room after each skate, having a drink and telling stories from his past. He had played in the NHL briefly, and guys often gathered around him like he was a campfire. I remember playing absolutely terrible during one game in Kitchener and I knew he was going to blast me in the room between periods. He stormed into the locker room, looked at me, and yelled, "Davis, the only draft you're going to see is the draught at the American Tavern." The American was a local watering hole in Waterdown and his point was clear: pick up your intensity.

One thing that sticks out about my hockey career is that when I was bad, I was extremely bad. Between Swervin Ervin and Spud, I learned how to deal with yelling coaches, how to battle through adversity, and, most of all, how to be resilient. After the game, these coaches would ask about my family and could separate the game from my personal life. I have always tried to do this in my own coaching as a result.

Earlier in the year, I had injured my knee pretty badly and I was out for five weeks. I came back healthy and ended up having a really good season. I was having a great series against Stratford in the playoffs, but I separated my shoulder in the last game of the series and they eliminated us. My year was finished and I had the summer to fully rehab my shoulder and get ready for the OHL Draft. I was ready to prove my doubters wrong, and I felt like I was ready for the next step.

The OHL Draft was held at Maple Leaf Gardens that year, and this time, I remembered to wear a suit. *The Hockey News* rated me one of the top 20 players in the draft, and I expected to be a first-round pick. I filled out my draft profile and I said that I would report to all teams but one, the Sudbury Wolves. My memory was long and I wanted to prove them wrong. Over the summer, I went to a couple Elite NCAA showcase skates in Buffalo so that I had a backup plan if the OHL Draft went poorly. I always figured my playing style was more suited to the U.S. game, and I loved watching NCAA sports. If I went to an NCAA school, I could watch football games on Saturdays and play hockey on a full athletic scholarship. Plus, it would give me time to put on weight and mature, as I still only weighed 155 pounds.

The first overall pick in the 1995 OHL Draft was Daniel Tkaczuk, and he was sitting right in front of me when he was selected. My turn was coming soon, so I prepared myself for the walk to the floor. The first round passed and I wasn't selected. The second, third, and fourth rounds went by, and I told my dad that I wanted to go home. My agent said that I would be picked soon, so stay and meet the team that drafts you. The Kingston Frontenacs selected me in the sixth round, and I was furious. I shook hands and put on the jersey, but I had no intention of ever playing in the OHL.

My pride was hurt and I was going to prove everyone wrong once again. My story would take a different turn a few months later, but at this moment in time, I was outraged. Only 14 players who were picked ahead of me in the 1995 OHL Draft finished with more career OHL points than I did. But, hey, but who's counting, right?

CHAPTER 4
LEAVING FOR THE WEEKEND
(Kingston Frontenacs, 1995–96)

The summer of 1995 was much different than any other summer I had experienced before. I was on the ice a lot more, and I attempted to work out to the best of my ability using the meager equipment I had access to. My workouts were designed around the high-tech, sand-filled, old-school Weider weight system in the basement of my parents' house. My goal was to get up to 160 pounds for the upcoming season in order to give myself the best opportunity possible and to prove I belonged in Kingston. The same Red Hot Chili Peppers album echoed in the background during every one of my workouts. July flew by and it was getting closer to my first Ontario Hockey League training camp. I would be going for a two-day skate, and I wasn't nervous at all because I had no plans on signing with Kingston. The OHL has a rule that you can only be in a team's training camp for 48 hours, and after that, you have to sign a contract or go home. This process allows you to keep your NCAA hockey eligibility and maintain your amateur status. If your name appears on a game sheet at any time, you lose the opportunity to play NCAA hockey. The time at training camp is essentially limited to a weekend of intrasquad games and practices. My plan was to go to Kingston with my dad, skate, and then return home to pursue my goal of playing at Princeton, Boston University, or any of the other schools sending me recruitment letters.

My dad and I left for Kingston at the end of August. I had packed all of my hockey equipment and a duffle bag consisting of a toothbrush, a golf shirt, khaki shorts, two t-shirts, and two pairs of underwear. It was just enough stuff to last the two days of training camp. When I arrived, I was set up with a billet family for the weekend and my dad stayed at a local hotel. The first day of camp was a little overwhelming to say the least. It was the fastest hockey I had ever played, and I struggled to keep up with the pace. As I mentioned before, there is a huge jump in ability due to size, strength, and speed at each level of the game. Although I had a very good year in Junior B, this level of hockey was much different. I was an average skater, but as the weekend went on, I started to catch up. I was happy with how I was playing and enjoying the new challenge of the OHL. Going into the weekend, I knew that the team had signed their underage player, as well as their first round pick. Spots were limited, but it didn't matter to me. My goal for the training camp was to play well and to show the team they'd missed the boat. After that, I would head home Sunday night and get ready for another year in Cambridge. Looking back on my mindset, it really didn't make any sense. Kingston was the team that drafted me, so why was I mad at them?

The advantage the Ontario Hockey League has over the NCAA is that it exposes their players to a high level of hockey and the bright lights of the junior game before players are even NCAA eligible. At training camp, fans sat in the stands and evaluated the new draft picks, young kids asked for autographs, and reporters conducted interviews for the next day's newspaper. Oh, and girls looked at you differently, even if you were six foot four and a rail thin 155 pounds with a concave chest. You fell into the trap of being a big deal, and priorities shifted very quickly. On the second day of camp, I read the newspaper to see if the reporter had anything good to say about me and my performance so far. I was hoping for some attention and maybe even a photo in the paper. The other huge advantage the OHL had at that time was the perks. The mandatory full cage from Junior B was gone and on came the visor, along with team-issued gloves and unlimited tape, the team's Gatorade wasn't watered down anymore to cut costs, and it was actually mixed with clean ice. All things considered, my brain began to question my decision and whether I really wanted to wait a couple more years to play NCAA hockey. Did I want to go home to play two more years in Junior B and hope for an NCAA scholarship? It was a big decision, and OHL training camp essentially became a 48-hour wine-and-dine affair. When my time at training camp was over, I was called into the general manager's office for a players' meeting and a quick debrief of my weekend with the Kingston Frontenacs.

I can still remember standing in the hall of the old Kingston Memorial Gardens, waiting in line to see the general manager. Players would enter his office for their meeting and then exit through the back door to avoid the curious eyes waiting outside. You had no idea if the previous player had signed a contract or if they had just been released back to their junior team. As the line shortened, butterflies formed in my stomach. The door eventually opened and I walked into the office. After a brief conversation, he told me I had impressed them at camp, and that they would like to sign me to an OHL contract. The coach encouraged me to talk to my parents and my agent and to let the team know by the end of the day. I stood up, thanked everyone in the room, and tried to contain my emotions. I wanted to maintain my composure and to make it look like the news wasn't that big a deal. After exiting the room, I found my dad and told him the exciting news. We proceeded to call my agent, Don Reynolds, to inform him that I would be signing a contract with the Kingston Frontenacs. Don worked out my school package and my contract details, and he agreed it was a good decision.

In those days, a school package was compensated by the round that you were drafted in. The goal was to give the players enough money to pay for their university degree when their OHL career was finished. A player would lose access to his school package money if he signed a pro hockey contract after he finished his OHL career. Basically, if you went to university immediately after you finished your four-year career, your school package kicked in right away and you received the agreed upon amount of money for each year you attended the university of your choice. A first-round pick in 1995 received between $6,000 and $8,000, on average, and all the top-ranked players received more money than the rest, but in my mind, it was a bit of a scam. It was very likely that a first-rounder would end up signing a pro contract, so their team would proabably never end up having to pay that $10,000 school package that was promised. On the flip side, any pick after the second round was a gamble, so the compensation level dropped significantly. I was drafted in the sixth round of that year's draft, but we were able to negotiate a little more money due to my NCAA interest. That still only paid me $3,000 a year for every year I attended university. Seeing as tuition was $5,000 at that time, along with living expenses, books, and food, I was barely getting a third of the total cost of my yearly education. Why didn't we negotiate a better deal? Because coaches and GMs had a lot of power at that time, and it was a take it or leave it proposition. The further along I got in my career, the more power these coaches had. It affected everything I did, from fighting to hazing, and only now can I understand how predators like Graham James, David Frost, and others who stayed hidden in the weeds existed. Signing a contract was just the tip of the iceberg. No was never an option. If you didn't want to sign the contract you were offered, you were gone and you may never get the opportunity to play in the OHL again. The contract I was offered was deemed to be fair at the time, and if I had said no, the team would have moved on to the next player. There was no shortage of players dreaming to play in the OHL. Things have recently changed to benefit current OHL players and they are moving in the right direction. The contracts are essentially universal, and there is less of a negotiation between the team and the player after the draft. Most of the guys we recruited during my last year at the University of Western were arriving with an average of $10,000 a year in tuition money. They were collecting housing expenses and book money well after they claimed their yearly tuition. I missed the boat on that one.

━━━

After I signed my OHL contract, I called my mom from the arena parking lot. It was one of the toughest calls I have ever had to make. I grew up a bit of an introvert, so I was always close to my parents, and very comfortable at home. You spend your entire life in the car with your parents, driving to games and practices, and suddenly you are 500 kilometres away, living with strangers. My mom picked up the phone and I explained to her that I had made the team, and I wouldn't be coming home. The news was shocking to her, to say the least. The team placed me with the same billets from training camp, and I needed my mom to pack my belongings and drive them to Kingston. School started in two days, and I needed more than two t-shirts and a couple of pairs of underwear. It was the first phone call of many to my mom over the years, asking her for something ASAP. It was also the first of many abrupt changes in my life.

The Frontenacs played a couple of memorable exhibition games before the season started. We had a walk-on player named Dylan Taylor, who was 18 years old and of diminutive size. He fought four or five times that training camp, trying to make the team, and it was an eye-opener to see the competition ahead. After removing the school package part of things, the rookies were now on an equal playing level, each trying his best to gain the coaches' trust. The Peterborough Petes had an 18-year-old walk-on as well that season, Shawn Thornton, who would end up winning a Stanley Cup many years later. During training camp, these two players had a couple of the best fights I have ever seen, as they were both doing anything they could to make their respective team. This was an era in hockey when players who wanted to make the team might have had to fight four or five times in one week to do so. Both of the players made it and went on to be big parts of their teams' successes that upcoming season. For me, it was a wake-up call that I needed to step up my play if I expected to stay in the league and to continue my dream of playing at the highest level possible. I also realized I didn't really like the idea of fighting.

The rest of my preseason was uneventful and I ended up being the odd man out to start the season. This was normal, and as a rookie you were expected to sit out as many games as you played. I eventually learned that some first-year players would untie their skates halfway through a game and keep their helmet undone so their head wouldn't get sore. Others would sneak snacks onto the bench and play scoreboard bingo with the rookie sitting beside them. You would each pick a number and if the clock stopped at a time that included that number, you'd win. If you guessed eight, and the clock stopped at 5:48, you won the bet. The wager would be a dollar and you would keep a running score throughout the game. All of this was to distract you from the fact you were never going to get on the ice. Sometimes when the score would get out of hand, you would fear the tap on your shoulder to go fight a rookie on the other team. Basically in a 6–1 game, two guys who hadn't had a single shift, who are freezing cold, and who haven't had an impact on the game are told to go fight each other. It makes a lot of sense, doesn't it? We would cheer for the game to stay close so we would never have to be put in that situation.

People will sometimes ask me about my stance on fighting and might be surprised to find out I support it. It helps to police those who take liberties with other players and who attempt to injure their opponents. In other words, it prevents someone from doing something stupid without real consequence. What I am against is the staged fighting that I previously talked about. Having two kids who haven't played a single shift fight at the end of a 6–1 game to "set the tone" is prehistoric. So much of the anxiety and depression that came with the enforcer role years ago was from sitting in your hotel room the night before a game knowing you were going to have to fight a guy who you didn't even know. Many of these players would have to check the game notes when they arrived at the arena, just to see who they would have to fight that night and to muster up the necessary aggression needed to do it. It made no sense at the time and it makes no sense now. Fighting is in the game because hockey is a physical sport and it eventually leads to confrontation. When you play someone within your division six times a year, you develop a hatred towards them. If a fight breaks out in the heat of the moment, that is completely within the confines of the game. As someone who did not play an overly physical game, I knew there were times that I would have to drop the gloves because of something that happened during the game. I think the OHL is close to getting it right with their fight limitation rules, and they are learning from their past mistakes, and having a multi-talented player like Tom Wilson on the ice for the Washington Capitals sets the tone on what is acceptable during the game while also protecting a player like Alexander Ovechkin.

On the first weekend of my rookie season, I got very lucky. I received a huge break and to this day, I wonder what my career would have been if it hadn't happened. We started our season off on a road trip to the Soo, and I was a healthy scratch. I had to work out in the hotel gym in the morning with the other players who weren't in that night's lineup. The regulars slept in their rooms and carried out their pregame routines. After my workout, I showered and headed to the rink on the team bus. We arrived at the old Soo Memorial Gardens, and I watched the warm-up from the stands, with some freshly popped popcorn. Afterwards, the assistant coach found me in the hallway and told me that our import player from the Czech Republic had injured his groin during warm-up. He asked me to get dressed quickly; I was now in the lineup. It's a moment I will never forget. I played a few shifts in the first period, and I scored my first OHL goal. By the end of the game, I had scored a hat trick, and I was the first star of the game. It was a great feeling, and I secured myself in the lineup for the rest of the season. My moment came and I took advantage of the opportunity.

Unfortunately, my first major OHL injury happened in Barrie a few months later. We were playing in the old Dunlop Street Arena, as Barrie was still waiting for their new rink to be completed. It was a small arena and Barrie had a pretty physical team. On an early shift in the second period, I was backchecking into my zone well behind the play and an opposing player grabbed the back of my shoulder and slew-footed me, causing me to fall backwards and hit my head on the ice. A slew foot is when someone kicks a player's feet forward and simultaneously presses their upper body backwards, causing them to fall dangerously to the ice. Other than a hit from behind, I think it is one of the dirtiest plays in hockey. My entire world turned fuzzy and everything moved in slow motion. When people ask me what a concussion feels like, this is how I would describe it: your world turns a shade of grey, you hear nothing but a buzzing sound, your surroundings seem to be in perfect slow motion, and you feel like you are in your own world. Your first instinct is to get to your feet, act normal, and to try to get to your bench without the other team figuring out you are hurt. Every step is a challenge to get your equilibrium, and the bench seems to get farther with each stride that you take. Every concussion I had seemed like déjà vu.

When I eventually got to the bench, I told our trainer that I thought something was wrong with me. In those days, the word "trainer" was very generous. Very few of the training staff, if any, had any medical training. The requirement was a weekend course in sports injuries or a first aid certificate. The training staff usually consisted of a single person who doubled as the team equipment manager. Our trainer at the time, Bobby, had this dual role, and he had been with Kingston for years. He was a gruff older man who kept his dentures in a cup after most games, and he did his best. In reality, he did not have a clue about how to treat a major or minor hockey injury. He managed a local hotel in town, and his hockey trainer's role was a seasonal position. When Bob came down to see me on the bench, he asked, "What seems to be wrong with you?" I looked up and said, "I think I hit my head on the ice, but I'll be okay. I just need a couple of minutes." Bob looked into my eyes, asked a couple of questions, and told the coach I was good to go back on the ice. I hopped over the boards and joined the power play for the next shift. I was in a total fog and after 45 seconds, I came back to the bench and puked everywhere. I could not stop throwing up. Any motion or light from the arena caused me to throw up again. The trainer told me to sit still until the period ended and he would "reassess" me during the intermission. Heaven forbid I interrupted the game and they actually took me to the dressing room right away. At that time, a concussion was treated the same as a pulled groin.

The period ended and I skated on my own towards our dressing room. Barrie's team doctor looked at me in the hallway and asked a couple of concussion related questions. I had no recollection of going back on the ice for that one shift during the power play and that was enough for him to tell me that my night was done. How does a trainer in 1995 deal with a player who has been ruled out of the game? These were my instructions: "After we go out for the second period, take your equipment off, try to shower, turn off the dressing room lights, and lay down in the shower until we get back in. I'll lock the door so nobody bothers you. You shouldn't move around, so try and stay still." What? There I was on the shower floor, all by myself in the dark, trying not to move, and throwing up in the shower drain whenever I needed to. After the game, I somehow managed to undress, shower, and board the bus back to Kingston.

When we arrived in Kingston, Bob gave me four Tylenols (wrong), told me to drive straight home (wrong), and let my billets know they had to wake me up every three hours (almost got it). I wasn't cleared to practice for two whole days, and I ended up playing the following weekend. I guess I just had a first degree case of ignorance or a random case of food poisoning. So you might be thinking, *Why wouldn't you just tell the team that you weren't feeling right?* In the hockey world, there's a fine line between protecting yourself and protecting your spot in the lineup. I gained my spot in the lineup from an injured player, and I was not going to allow someone to do the same to me. The issue at that time was that there was never anyone to protect us from ourselves. Currently, the OHL has attempted to put proper protocols in place with the goal of protecting their players from returning to play too early. I wish I had access to that protection during my rookie season.

My second major injury of the season happened shortly after. In 1995, the OHL game of the week was a huge deal. For a limited number of weeks during the season, GlobalTV broadcasted one game per week. In early December, it was our time to have a game broadcast, and it was pretty special to be able to play for the people back home. It was also an opportunity of to show off my success to those who doubted me in Flamborough minor hockey. Maybe it was possible for a kid from Carlisle to make it to major junior hockey. I called everyone I knew to tell them that our game was going to be on TV on Saturday afternoon. It was exciting for me and I wanted to play well. During the second period of the game, I was standing in front of the net on the power play. Being in front of the net was something I was really good at, and it became my calling card. I averaged six or seven goals a year off my pants, shin pads, skates or off an easy rebound. It's not how, but how many, right? On this particular power play, the puck was passed back to the point to one of our defencemen, Chris Allen. Chris had an absolute laser and would go on to win hardest shot at the Top Prospects Game that year. I watched him wind up to shoot the puck, but I lost the location of the shot when a defenceman darted in front of me to clear the front of the net. When I managed to look around the defenceman's shoulder, I felt an explosion in my mouth and my lip went completely numb. I fell and blood pooled into my visor as soon as I hit the ice. When the trainer rushed onto the ice to help, he gave me a towel to put pressure on my lip to stop the bleeding. I stood up and skated off the ice as quick as I could. The viewers at home got to see a close-up of my face and visor covered in blood. It wasn't the impression I was looking to make on live TV, but at least I got a close-up, right?

When I walked into our trainer's room, the doctor said I would need 12 to 15 stitches to close the gap, but luckily I still had all of my teeth. I looked in the mirror and the cut went from my nose to my lip and I could see my teeth through my lip. The doctor injected the anesthetic into my mouth and started to stitch right away. At about stitch four, the entire arena, including the training room, went dark — not a ray of light in the entire building. The Kingston Memorial Gardens was ancient, and the power that was needed to broadcast the game overloaded the circuits and caused a blackout. It took the doctor 10 minutes to find a flashlight before he could continue to stitch. There was one tiny problem: they couldn't keep the flashlight still and the doctor couldn't see. The result? A 12-stitch scar that zigzags down my lip like it was sewn shut by a third grade student with shaky hands. I returned to the ice for the third period and finished the game. It was still on television after all, and people at home got to watch me play.

The off-ice part of the game is what I loved and what I still miss after all of these years. I loved the attention I was getting, I loved how I felt after a good game, and, most of all, I loved the camaraderie. If I could go to the rink with my equipment already in a dressing room stall, have someone else tie my skates, play for 10 minutes or less, and come back into the room for a cold beverage and good conversation, then I'd sign up tomorrow. I could stay in my half equipment after a game or practice and banter with the boys for hours. Our dressing room in Kingston was a lot of fun, and the off-ice atmosphere was awesome. Everything was novel to me as a rookie, so I was always anticipating pranks or shenanigans. One day before practice, we sawed another player's stick so that it was three-quarters of the way cut through the shaft. You have to remember that this was a time when your game stick was worth $30, not $300. Practice started and the first drill was going terribly. The entire team couldn't make a tape-to-tape pass or do anything right. The coach blew his whistle and snapped. He screamed that we would start the drill over, and if we still couldn't make a pass, the whole team would go to the boards for a skate. Who do you think was at the front of the line for the first repetition when we restarted the drill? On the whistle, the player with the broken stick made a pass, he skated around the zone and received the puck back on his stick. He took a slapshot and the stick snapped into the air and he fell flat on his face. The coach immediately figured out what had happened and the entire team skated until we puked.

On my first overnight road trip, I was introduced to the shoecheck. The shoecheck is an old hockey tradition that consists of putting some sort of sauce or condiment on someone's shoes at a meal without them knowing. The team would be sitting at a table in a restaurant, eating a nice meal and enjoying some small talk. The older players would designate a target and try to distract him from the imminent attack. At the same time, a player would slip under the table, crawl on their hands and knees the length of the table, spread the condiment on his victim, then reverse crawl on the dirty floor under the table back to their original seat. The entire team would then tap their glass with a fork — the signal for everyone to check their shoes, pretending like they had no idea what had just happened. The target of the attack would look down and find ketchup, mustard, tomato sauce or mayonnaise on their expensive dress shoes, and the table would erupt in cheers and laughter. Players would play stupid and ask around, "Who did that? How did that happen?" Shoechecks were a staple throughout the year, and one player was even targeted three times in a single meal at East Side Mario's. The downside of the shoecheck was that you could never enjoy a good meal. Also, you would have to rush off the bus to get a seat facing the entire restaurant for better surveillance, and you would some-times have to eat holding a spoon, using it like a rearview mirror to see any approaching perpetrators. As the story goes, one of my good friends play-ing for Oshawa at the time shoechecked David Branch at the Memorial Cup, by crawling under the table past the feet of unsuspecting tournament sponsors and league executives. It brought down the house. As always, we thought it was hilarious, but others outside the game never understood the immaturity of it. We referred to these non-hockey people as "civilians."

As in, "I was on the floor of the restaurant with a ketchup-filled spoon in my hand, and all of these civilians were staring at me."

Hockey continued to go well and I was having the time of my life. I was enjoying signing autographs and being recognized around town. Rookies are generally just happy to be in the OHL, but I was fortunate to be getting a lot of ice. As the year progressed, the pranks and stories were too numerous to remember. A player's car was filled entirely with packing styrofoam, to the point that the player couldn't even open his door to drive home. Our assistant captain was from Newfoundland, and the coach had to tell him that although it was a great idea, he would have to take the chains off the tires of his car, as it was illegal in our province. Phone calls were made throughout the year from "NHL scouts," informing different players that an NHL team was very interested. These "scouts" would continue to ask the players some very personal questions. You knew it was most likely a prank call from a teammate with nothing to do but you were afraid to hang up just in case it was legit. There were many times when a real NHL scout had to call a player twice because the player just assumed it was a fake phone call and hung up on them. Without cell phones and call display, we could entertain ourselves pretty creatively.

Kangaroo Court was one of my favourite things in the world. If something questionable happened or a player was caught breaking the hockey code in public, Kangaroo Court would be called into session. Most of the time you had no idea what had happened or if you were the one to be called to court. The captain was usually the lead prosecutor and the player charged with the crime would have to defend himself in front of the team. Charges usually consisted of something female or girlfriend related. Holding hands in public, a girlfriend wearing your jersey, not getting a veteran his Gatorade, hiding condiments on the bus, or having a bad haircut were just some reasons of what could get you a date in court. The verdict 99.9 percent of the time was guilty, and you would have to do something stupid for the rest of the week. The whole process was hilarious, and it distracted us from the monotony of playing junior hockey. You went into battle every day with these guys, so you had to learn how to laugh at each other and yourself. If you couldn't laugh at yourself, hockey would find a way to humble you very quickly.

It was my third consecutive year as a rookie, and I looked forward to this being my last initiation for a while. By this point, initiations in the OHL were still going strong, and it was widespread across the league. We had a reasonable group of veterans, so I wasn't too worried. As I mentioned earlier, there is always one veteran player on every team who is miserable and who wants retribution for what happened to him in his rookie year. Hopefully, the captain and the assistants can get him to calm down and protect others from this stupidity. Our leadership group in Kingston was great, and our captain, Mark Moro, was in charge. He was an OHL heavyweight, which made him an authority in our dressing room. The rookies still had to load and unload the bus for each road game that season, which included hauling the equipment trunk, skate sharpener, water, and sticks to and from the arena. Once in a while, some veterans would want their bags carried out to the bus and loaded. You would kindly oblige rather than pay the price later. Rookies always sat two to a seat near the front of the bus, always got their meals last, and condiments were a privilege you received if you were lucky. Sleeping two to a seat was especially tough for me on longer road trips but for the most part, Kingston was a great travel team with close road trips within our division.

Every Tuesday night we were given extended curfew (11:30 p.m.!) and we were allowed to go to watch a discounted movie. Rookies would have to stand up and tell a joke to the crowd before the movie started or we were told to laugh really loud at a part in the movie that wasn't funny at all. These initiations always stunned the crowd, but it was funny to watch the players get anxious over these small pranks. One week we had to go to the movies in our jock, underwear, and a t-shirt, while wearing our helmet and gloves. We stood in line for popcorn, acting like everything was normal. When we got to the front of the line, we would ask the server if they had any cleaner for your visor or plastic tape for your shinpads. The servers were stunned, and very few civilians found it even remotely funny. It didn't matter to us, as we found the humour in it.

Little did the veterans know that my Junior C days at the local IGA had prepared me for this.

The "hotbox" initiation was reserved for the longest road trip of the year and was a yearly tradition for all of the rookies in the league. This tradition has become a hot topic of debate over the last couple of years and if you ask 95 percent of the players from my time in the league, they would say they participated in a least one hot box experience. In Kingston, it was planned for the North Bay trip, as it was a five-hour bus ride. We boarded the bus after the game and ate dinner while a movie played on the TVs. Swiss Chalet accounted for 80 percent of the meals in the OHL, and I can still taste the soggy fries and cold, greasy chicken that had been ready to eat 30 minutes before the game ended. The only good meal we ever had was from the Penalty Box in Windsor, and the boys circled it on their calendar.

After the meal, the rookies were called one by one to the back of the bus where the veterans sat. Each of us stood up, took off all of our clothes, tied a skatelace around our genitals, and walked to the back of the bus. During that "walk of shame," veterans slapped us on the ass and had the opportunity to pull on the string around our genitals. Veterans who were treated poorly in their rookie year would take the time to yank as hard as they could, laughing sadistically in the process and forcing you to bite your lip to mask the pain. You didn't want to show weakness because that put a target on your back. Most of my teammates refused to pull the string or just pretended to in order to appease the group. Unfortunately, not everyone was that hospitable. When toxic culture is given room to breathe, it can last for generations. When we arrived at the back of the bus, the veterans told us to sit down and make them laugh within the next 20 seconds. If you couldn't make them laugh, you would have to go stand in the washroom and shut the door. Nobody ever succeeded in making the older guys laugh, so we were each sent into the bathroom with whoever was in there before you. This went on until every rookie was shoved in the bathroom completely naked. Obviously, if the veterans liked you, you would be called over towards the end of the process. It was called the hotbox because the driver was told to turn up the heat to its highest level and the bathroom door was locked shut. All of our clothes were tied in a giant knot and thrown into the bathroom. We had seven rookies that year, so it was a traffic jam to say the least. If you managed to get your clothes untangled and get yourself dressed, you could come out of the bathroom. It was nearly impossible. We spent over three hours in that bathroom, and I remember it like it was yesterday. We secretly managed to get the small window open a crack, so we could get a bit of fresh air and continue to breathe. It was not a lot of fun, but we managed to unite as rookies to survive the ordeal. We just told ourselves it was normal to be naked, sweaty, and squished in an overheated bus bathroom for three hours. We tried to calm claustrophobic teammates down and instructed them to breathe. It was considered a rite of passage, and nobody spoke up unless they wanted to be beaten. We got through it together and it was a continuation of my indoctrination into the cult of hockey. After all, passing out in a bus bathroom with my naked teammates would make me a better hockey player, wouldn't it?

Was the hotbox incident a form of abuse? I ask myself this question all the time, especially as news continues to come out about former players claiming this (and other incidents) as forms of mistreatment. It may very well have been abuse, but I think it is based on your perception of the situation. You might be wondering how I can even question whether or not this was sexual abuse. Remember, I had played Junior C and Junior B hockey before this, so I was led to believe that you treated the veterans with respect, you did what they asked you to do, and eventually you would be in charge and you would lead the new group of rookies. I was essentially brainwashed by this point, so my opinion was skewed. Nudity was normal to me, and at no time in my career did I ever feel threatened or unsafe. Initiation taught players humility. It didn't matter if you were a first-rounder or a 10th-round pick, you were treated the exact same. Wrapping up your first year was like completing an apprenticeship for a job. Initiations like having to pick up pucks in warm-up in front of three thousand fans make it clear where you stand in the hockey hierarchy. The common sentiment among veteran players was, "Know your role, Rookie." As far as the coaches go, I don't blame most of them either. Maybe I should, but I don't. Let me be clear, they knew what was happening. Coaches always sat at the front of the bus, they never turned around, and they rarely used the bathroom. They pretended to be watching the movie and acted like they couldn't hear anything at the back of the bus — but we were on a 60-seat coach bus, not a cruise ship. They may have pleaded ignorance, but like everything else going on with the team, they knew exactly what was happening, they just chose to ignore it, and this, too, was part of the tradition. Coaches assumed ultimate authority over every part of our life, so how could they miss this?

So what were coaches supposed to do? Every team in the league had the same rituals, and initiations had been going on for decades. Half of the coaches in the league had probably been in that hotbox during their career as well. It was going to take one coach to break the cycle, but nobody was prepared to do that, as their only focus was to win hockey games. Hockey is an old boys' network and nobody was ready for change. Much like I mentioned earlier with the Akim Aliu story, I'm sure many of these coaches have the same regret that I do: that they never stood up for change and seized the opportunity to be a real leader. To be clear, I never liked being initiated and some of the pranks were just weird, but I always wanted to be a good teammate and I, like many others, just did what I was told. An adult should have stepped in and protected us from ourselves. I spent most of my career looking around the room for the adults, but most of them preferred their role as the dictator feared by teenagers.

While writing about my experiences, I couldn't help but return to a rose-coloured conclusion: What happened to me occurred a quarter of a century ago. Certainly, my stories were outdated; I was dwelling on the past, and the game had drastically changed for the better. Right? These assumptions became part of my internal reasoning, in an optimistic attempt to gain closure. When I had the opportunity to read the *2020 CHL Report on Player Wellbeing*, my optimism disappeared.

The report was created by an Independent Review Panel (the "Panel") appointed by the CHL to review the current policies, procedures, and programs in the CHL. These topics related to hazing, abuse, harassment, bullying, and the allegations that players do not feel comfortable reporting off-ice incidents. To say that this report was shocking would be an understatement. The panel found that 21 years after my last OHL game, off-ice misconduct still exists in the CHL. Toxic culture is still the norm. Even worse, the panel found that modelling by senior members (i.e., owners, coaches, GMs, older players) and the general acceptance of these behaviours were the main reasons for this culture.

When reading through the documents, it was not surprising that the panel found CHL players became desensitized over time to these "toxic" actions and misconduct. Basically, this behaviour is still "normal" for the sport and young players just learn to deal with it. These were the feelings I wrestled with when I retired. The further I distanced myself from hockey, the higher the veil lifted, and I was embarrassed by what I saw, not only from myself, but from the people who shaped my adolescence. What I had deemed "normal" behaviour now looked much different. I finally accepted that I needed to make amends with the way I treated people during this time period, but I also needed somebody to apologize to me.

Let me be clear. The initial report, with recommendations, was followed up by a more detailed review by Rachel Turnpenney of Turnpenney Milne LLP, and there were no legal findings. Her job was to review if these policies and programs assisted in the protection of the players. There were a couple of key things that stood out to me in regard to current player safety. On page five of the report, Turnpenney states, "The first step is for the CHL and Member Leagues to focus on sustaining a healthy and positive culture. They must rethink their culture and the perceptions that exist about the CHL and the Member Leagues — whether those perceptions are true or not" (Turnpenney, 2022). There are numerous policies and programs that the CHL has put into place, and these policies are a clear sign that they are attempting to address some important issues. I personally feel that as a league, the CHL is trying to evolve into something much better — but they face one major issue. While the CHL is the world's largest developmental hockey league, it is divided into three separate leagues: the OHL, the WHL, and the QMJHL. These leagues consist of 60 teams total, with eight of those being American. So even though the league has a "national" championship in the Memorial Cup, the CHL still only acts as an umbrella organization, and it has not mandated uniformity among the leagues. This means that each league has implemented the Player Wellbeing Programs differently as they each have varying ideas on how to best address these issues. Therefore, there is no uniformity in the program.

The most damaging area of the Turnpenney report, for me, is what everyone knew all along. She states that, "In terms of initial perceptions, the CHL and the Member Leagues present as a mostly white, male organization that lack diversity in terms of equity seeking groups at the Member League level, and the management level within each entity" (Turnpenney, 2022). So how can you address culture and change the outlook of your league and the future of junior and professional hockey if everyone looks, breathes, and acts the same way? It's not possible, and it's easy to figure out why a negative systemic culture exists and why these behaviours are condoned and tolerated. Essentially, those in positions of power, those who control the culture, do not know any better as they were treated in a similar manner. Are coaches, GMs, and staff willing to shift the perceptions and experiences of their organizations?

The evidence that things are still broken is reflected in the surveys conducted in the Independent Review Panel report. In almost all of the surveys, there were discrepancies between what the players, families, and billets found versus the opinions of the team staff. For example, 41 percent of CHL families feel there is a problem with harassment but only 19 percent of GMs feel the same way. Twenty-four percent of players feel that there is a problem with discrimination but only 16 percent of CHL GMs think there is an issue. Why is there such a big gap? This is the issue facing the game of hockey, and it's a problem that has been around since my time in the league. The people in power positions can turn a blind eye or see the issues at hand as being much smaller than they are. Ignorance by association is their method of change. When players were asked why they were afraid to report an issue, they often stated they were afraid of retaliatory conduct or lack of consequences. There is a code of silence and players are afraid to break their loyalty to the team. Do you think I wanted to risk reporting anything I saw to a coach, giving him an excuse to release me or to form a pattern of retribution through withholding icetime or opportunity? Of course not. So until players feel like there is a safe way to report issues without facing backlash, they are going to continue to stay silent.

Let me be clear, this isn't an issue with every team. The culture of each team varies from city to city, and I applaud those teams addressing this issue head-on. I currently work as one of three OHL Player Liaison Officers for the Guelph Storm. The other two liaisons are police officers within the city of Guelph. My job, as well as theirs, is to listen to the players, support them, and gain their trust in case an incident occurs. My role is to remain independent from the organization in reporting any issues, and I do not report these issues to the coach or GM. The team supports this initiative put in place by the league and encourages their approach to anonymity and the protection of their players. This is how the system should work, but this is one of 60 teams in the CHL. There is still a lot of work to be done — but it is never too late.

As far as the hotbox goes, it no longer has a place in the game, but I still think there is a role for safe initiation in the league. Too many kids come in cocky and expect the world at their feet. They expect to be on the power play because they were a first-rounder, they refuse to do anything extra, and they are entitled. Parents call the coach after games asking about ice time and they request trades when the going gets tough. If my mom ever called Brian Kilrea, he would've said, "Come pick him up. He can have all the ice time he wants at home." The hotbox and other similar traditions were created to foster a kind of humility that doesn't exist today. Life lessons of respecting your elders and having to learn patience and resilience are foreign now. They have been replaced by an attitude that says, "I deserve this," "I expect this," and "life is too difficult." I hope that we can find a middle ground where adversity and respect are valued in the game. How can we build team unity in a safe environment? I don't claim to have the answer, but I do hope engaging in this discussion allows us to find a better way.

The season continued and I had a great year. I ended with 30 goals, 18 assists, and 20 penalty minutes. More importantly, 10 of those penalty minutes were because of fights. I had slowly crept onto the NHL Draft boards and my agent at the time hinted that it might be a good idea to mix in a fight or two, and he would promote it to the teams that were interested. I picked my spots and I ended up doing just fine. I didn't enjoy it, and I always had trouble finding the aggression to do it. Fighting came easier to other players, but I always tried to fight at least twice a year, and that was good enough for me. My centreman that year was Colin Chaulk, and he was one of the best passers I ever played with. He was a great guy and he made my job of scoring goals very easy. Whenever I was open, Colin would find me, and I never had a problem with finishing after that. He was the perfect centreman for my style of play and a big reason for my success.

By the end of the season, my agent was Allan Walsh. He was new on the scene and I was one of his first two clients. Agents are a funny bunch. If things are going well, you will be in constant contact with them, but as soon as things start going downhill, your number seems to be misplaced. Allan had been a part of the prosecution team of the O.J. Simpson case in L.A., but his first love was the game of hockey. He left L.A. and headed to Montreal to start his player agency. Like most players, I had a hard time getting a hold of my previous agent whenever I needed him. Numerous calls would go unanswered, and the NHL players occupied all of his time.

When I first met Allan, he could see that I was extremely frustrated. He seemed to be at every one of my games, and he actually cared about me as a person, so I made the switch and became one of his first clients. Plus, I got unlimited information on the O.J. case that sealed the deal. I left my old representation as I wasn't officially bound to the contract with them anyway. Allan is now a big-time agent in the NHL with Octagon Sports, and he represents some of the biggest names in hockey. I like to think I played a small part in his success, with the emphasis on "small."

The season ended and we lost to a strong Peterborough Petes team. As a rookie, you look forward to the season ending and going home to see your friends. My year had been memorable, but there was something special about sleeping in your own bed and living in your own house. I had left unexpectedly seven months earlier, so I was excited to finally return home. Allan told me that teams were very interested in me and that I should attend the 1996 NHL Draft in St. Louis. When I arrived at the draft, I could meet the teams and interview with them in person. Two months after arriving back home, my parents and I packed up the car and headed for an exciting vacation to St. Louis, Missouri.

CHAPTER 5

FRESH CUT FRIES, POOLSIDE EDDIE, AND A GRINDING SUMMER

(NHL Draft, 1996)

We arrived at our hotel in St. Louis three nights before the draft, and I interviewed with seven or eight teams over the course of two days. Many of the interviews involved sitting in front of 10 or more scouts while I tried to answer the general manager's questions. The hardest part of the interview was trying to focus on the questions without getting distracted by thoughts like, *Is that really Scotty Bowman?* It was an intimidating process but one that prepared me for job interviews in the future. My heroes in hockey and people I idolized growing up were sitting across from me, asking me questions, like, "What would you do if a building was on fire and there were three people inside, but you could only carry two of those people out safely?" You walked out of the interview questioning every answer you gave. I can still remember eating lunch in the lobby of the hotel with my agent, and this enormous kid walked by.

I asked Allan, "Who's that guy?" Allan answered, "Some kid from Slovakia who played in the WHL. He's apparently climbing up the draft boards." It was Zdeno Chara.

It must have been over 100 degrees outside on draft day, and the humidity was awful. The walk from the hotel to the arena was three minutes long but I was drenched by the time I got there. My agent told me the previous day that he expected me to get drafted from the fourth round on, so don't worry about getting there too early. I translated that statement into, no rush and take your time, you'll end up being a sixth rounder. My parents and I arrived at the draft and much to my delight, the snack bar was open. I bought a tray of fries, loaded on the ketchup, and headed down to find a seat. We sat near the top of the upper bowl and I scanned the arena to take in the whole process. It was surreal to be a part of all of this and I had to pinch myself a couple of times. By the time we took our seats, the draft was around the 70th pick, so I had time to soak it all in. With three fries remaining, I heard something I will never forget. "With the eighty-fifth pick of the NHL Draft, the Washington Capitals select Justin Davis." I was 18 years old and I had finally made it.

I walked down to the draft floor but I couldn't feel my legs. I shook hands with all of the scouts and then the general manager, David Poile. The team rushed me backstage where I got my photo taken and went through a couple of media interviews. The team invited my family to their post-draft party at the hotel, where I got to meet the coach, Jim Schoenfeld. I had a huge smile on my face the entire time, and I will never forget that day. Little did I know at that time that the work had just begun. The team gave me my individual workout plan and told me I would be spending the summer in Maryland at their team complex. Their goal was to make me stronger, to make me a better skater, and to help me become a complete hockey player. We drove back to Carlisle the next day, and I was excited to get started on the next phase of my career.

I arrived in Washington, D.C., in early July, and I was driven to the townhouse complex I would be staying at for the entire summer. It was a beautiful building, and our condo had three bedrooms with a pool area nearby.

My roommates rolled in later on, and I had never met any of them before. Matt Lahey lived across the hall and he played for the rival Peterborough Petes. My roommates were Chad Cavanaugh from the Sudbury Wolves and Jeff McNeil from the Spokane Chiefs. We all got along great and the whole summer felt like an episode of MTV's *The Real World*. We would get up three days a week at 6 a.m. and head to the U.S. Naval Base in Annapolis, Maryland, for a track workout before it got too hot. After breakfast, we would head to the gym for a one-hour workout and a 20-lap swim. The day would end with an hour of skating and shooting at the team practice facility, and we wrapped up most nights in the hot tub. We were bagged by the end of the week, but we always managed to enjoy some cocktails around the pool. This cycle continued for eight weeks of the summer.

One Friday night in the middle of July, we took our team-issued rental car, a Ford Taurus, out for a group dinner. Dinner led to a couple of drinks, which led us to stay out much later than we should have, and on the way home we ruined the car. We were driving a little too fast for a rental Ford Taurus and veered off a sharp corner, dragging the car for 10 metres along the guardrail. The sparks of the metal lit up the night, and the guardrail left a huge scrape on the side of the car. We continued the drive home, went to sleep, and figured we would deal with the aftermath in the morning. Have you ever pictured something one way, but in reality, it's much worse than you thought? The rental car was a complete mess. We had to explain what happened to our team chaperone (an assistant GM) the next morning and it eventually got fixed without much trouble. I had never been more anxious for a conversation; I thought the team would send us all home immediately. Little did I know, it was just a warm-up for future incidents to come.

Most days we would head to the pool before dinner to float and relax. After a while, we began to notice a five-foot-four, 140-pound leather-skinned man walking into the pool area daily at exactly 4 p.m. sharp. He would be carrying a cooler with 12 beers in one hand and a boombox in the other. His name was Eddie and he was a miniature, drunken version of Jeff Foxworthy. Eddie would drink those 12 beers in under two hours and serenade the pool area with "Waterfalls" and "Creep" from the latest TLC album. At the pool, every day was Groundhog Day, and I'm sure Eddie is still sitting there having a cold one.

Matt Lahey from across the hall was one of my favourite people from that summer, and we ended up playing together much later. "Laser" was a piece of work, and he made all of us laugh constantly. He hated the sun, loved tattoos, enjoyed Friendly's ice cream, and he was always reading about something. Most days you would find him under a blanket in a dark room, reading a book with a lip full of chewing tobacco. Matt was one of the best hockey players I ever played with. He had great hands, he was a great skater, and he could fight. His biggest issue for most of his career was his battle with his weight. Matt started the summer program at 235 pounds, and Washington asked him to lose 10 pounds before training camp. Laser worked hard, but ended up weighing in at 236 pounds for the start of training camp, which did not impress the team. Years later, when we played together in junior, one of our coaches burst into the room after a weigh in and yelled, "Laser! There are two things keeping you out of the NHL, a knife and a fork." The room erupted, and Matt had a little smile on his face. He never took himself seriously, and he was one of the best teammates I ever had. Unfortunately, Matt passed away a few years ago, much too soon, but I will never forget him and the time we had together.

By the end of the summer, I was in the best shape of my life. I returned home to rest for a couple of days and to prepare for my first NHL training camp. The summer had been a blur, as the weekly workouts left very little time for anything else, but I had had the opportunity to skate and work out with new friends and my idols from the NHL. Players I had watched on TV months before would be sitting beside me at the practice facility, asking me if I wanted a drink of water. It was surreal, but as the summer progressed, I started to believe that I belonged here. I was confident that I could make a big impression, and I excitedly flew back to Washington to start my first NHL training camp.

Back then, your fitness testing was on the first day of training camp. Bloodwork, body fat tests, EKGs, and body analysis were done in the morning, followed by VO2 max testing and the Wingate testing in the early afternoon. For the VO2 max test, trainers hook you up to a breathing tube and attach numerous sensors to your body. You start walking at a snail's pace on flat ground, and every minute the speed and incline of the treadmill increases. By the time you reach 16 minutes, you are sprinting uphill with a group of athletic therapists standing behind you, ready to catch you when you fall off the treadmill. The VO2 test measures how much oxygen your body consumes when you are exercising at your maximum work rate. The Wingate is a test that measures your anaerobic leg power, as hockey is an anaerobic sport. After a brief warm-up on an exercise bike, you are given a five second warning before you start pedalling as fast as you can. When the test begins, a weight or restriction is added, which provides an increased workload, and you can barely pedal by the end of the test. It's 30 seconds of hell that measures your anaerobic capacity and lactic threshold. The day finishes off with max bench press, max pull ups, and max weighted dips, along with some agility drills. When you get back to your hotel room, you can barely move.

On day two of training camp, the ice sessions began. It was common practice to bring your skates back to the hotel each day so that they would dry out properly, as moisture in dressing rooms during training camp is high. The heat outside combined with the number of players participating creates a climate that just doesn't allow things to dry very well. So it was during the preparation for my first skate of training camp that I realized I had left my skates back at the hotel. What a meathead move. Here I am ready to make an impression on the scouting staff, and I don't even have a pair of skates to wear. After a panicked search, one of my friends coming off of the first skate said I could borrow his. The problem was, they were CCMs, and I wore Bauer skates. At that time, skates were very different and they had different levels of pitch. CCMs were more forward leaning and they were difficult to wear if you had never worn them before. For a kid whose weakness was skating, looking like Happy Gilmore on day one of his first training camp was not a positive. I managed to make it through the skate that day, but it was all I could do to stay on my feet. I felt like I was wearing high heels on the ice. My skates arrived later that day, and I was better prepared for the intrasquad game.

When you participate in your first training camp, you are in awe of the NHL players. At that time, Washington had Peter Bondra, Joe Juneau, Adam Oates, Chris Simon, Olaf Kolzig, and my personal favourite in my second camp, Bill Ranford. I was a huge Edmonton Oilers fan, and shooting on Bill Ranford, the goalie who had led the Oilers to the Stanley Cup six years earlier and who won the Conn Smythe in the process, was surreal. I laughed at myself during warm-up drills because we were supposed to be hitting the goalies with shots to get them prepared, and I was scoring at will. I was ringing shots off the bar and silently celebrating each goal as the goalies barely managed to move. So much for trying to get warmed up. In my first scrimmage, the other team had a QMJHL league heavyweight who had just set the league record for penalty minutes in the previous season. As I was lined up beside him on a faceoff, I felt a tap on my pants. When I turned around, I realized it was Chris Simon. He was an NHL league heavyweight, and he told me to go sit down. I skated to the bench to watch them go at it, and I flinched with every power punch that was thrown. I scored on my second day of the intrasquad games and, overall, I thought I had a great camp. I met with David Poile, and after a brief conversation, I was told that I would be returning to junior hockey. I was excited to get back to Kingston and have an even better year than my first. I didn't know it at the time, but this would be the last time I loved the game for a very long time. Life was about to get very difficult.

CHAPTER 6
ONE-WAY TICKET TO THE SOO
(Kingston and the Soo Greyhounds, 1996–97)

When a player is having a terrible second season, there's a name for it: the sophomore slump. If I knew what was in store for me in my second year with the Frontenacs in the OHL, I would have renamed it the sophomore free fall. I returned from the Washington Capitals training camp just in time for the first game of the season. My best friend, Matt Bradley, was returned to the team from the San Jose Sharks at the same time I was, and we were both in the lineup that night. (Matt would go on to have a long, successful career in the NHL as a gritty, hardworking player.) We could've played better and we lost that first game, but we knew there was a long season ahead of us and this game was essentially meaningless. The next day in the *Kingston Whig-Standard*, our coach called Matt and me a pair of prima donnas and blamed the loss on our play. (Actually, the headline was "Prima Donnas Sink Frontenacs.") I wished

I knew that it would be the second worst headline referring to me that season, and it was going to get much worse.

The coach apologized later for making the comments in public, but the damage was done. I continued to struggle horribly, and I never fully regained my confidence. When you come back from the NHL, you expect to dominate and you tend to press in all areas of your game. When the points don't come, you get frustrated, and it feels like there is a 200-pound gorilla on your back. The worst part of slumping is when a rookie on the fourth line starts scoring, and you can barely register an assist. You feel the pressure build inside and it just overwhelms you.

Every couple of years I encounter the same situation with players I work with on the Guelph Storm. I end up taking the player out for dinner . . . and I tell the guy, "Just breathe." I explain that it happens to the best of us and you need to divert your attention elsewhere. Instead of sitting in bed each night, wishing the week away, waiting for Friday night so you have a chance to score and break out of the slump, read a book, work out, talk to your family; just get away from the game of hockey.

The team had game film review once a week, which is not the best activity for a player who is struggling. We would sit in the film room while the coach sped through the VHS tape to show us all the good and bad plays of the previous game. It was usually a brutal mistake followed by the question: "What were you thinking?" Even worse, our coach had a small laser pointer, and he would point the laser on the offending player all the way up the ice. "What were you thinking, JD?" he would say constantly. I would think, *Obviously I wasn't thinking, or we wouldn't be here* but I didn't have the balls to say it out loud. I should have just worn a red jersey that season, as the laser pointer was always following me. Your mistakes always looked worse on tape and it was embarrassing, especially when they showed it in slow motion. The anxiety of playing hockey continued to build after each weekend.

If last season was the best time of my life, this year was a nightmare. I was regularly a healthy scratch. Of course, the coaches rarely had any class. They made us sit and anxiously wait on a three-hour bus ride to find out our fate. When the bus would arrive at the game, everyone would walk down the aisle to exit the bus, and the coach would look at me and say, "JD, you're not playing tonight." It was a completely gutless process, and it wasn't right. Would it have killed the coach to tell me before I boarded the bus that I wasn't dressing that night? Would it have killed him to say that even though I wasn't playing tonight, I would be in the lineup tomorrow, so I should take the time to clear my head and relax? Nope. Complete mind games. And it's a major reason why so many of us are emotionless, with severe anxiety to this day. Without cell phones, we weren't able to tell our families we weren't playing until they arrived at the game. It was embarrassing and humiliating for the players who were scratched, and the coaches seemed to use that as motivation. Most of the time, my parents would sit with me and watch the game, even though I would barely say a word. Sometimes my dad would just drive home and leave me alone with my thoughts.

One weekend when we were playing a game in Guelph, the coach didn't give me a single shift even though I was dressed. Guelph is 20 minutes away from my hometown, and I had 40 people at the game cheering for me. He absolutely humiliated me. The coach made me sit there for three periods, knowing full well what was going on, and never communicated with me once. It was gutless, but to the coach, it was "motivation." Instead, I hated myself, hated the game, and felt depressed on the bus ride home. Junior hockey is slowly evolving and many of these coaches have either disappeared or been forced to change. I'm grateful that the abuse of our generation has led to some positive change.

One of the few reprieves we had from the stress of hockey was the time we spent together in the hotel on road trips. We would kill a huge part of the day going to the local mall, shopping, and causing chaos. A favourite pastime was going to the dollar store to buy Krazy Glue and gluing a loonie to the floor in the food court. A player would put glue on the loonie and then bend down to "tie his shoes." After the fake shoe tie, he would step on the loonie for a minute to ensure that it was secure. After the loonie was glued, players would sit at a table with some

Manchu Wok and watch the chaos erupt. What would people do for a loonie in the exquisite food courts of North Bay, Owen Sound, and Sudbury? People used credit cards, keys, and Swiss army knives (really) to try to scrape the dollar coin off the floor. Others would spend half an hour kicking it with their shoe or trying to free it with a lunch tray. One time in the Soo, we came back to the mall the next day to find an entire tiled section of the food court removed.

I woke up most mornings miserable and angry at the world. Most nights, I would sit by myself in my basement apartment, watching TV and trying to distract myself from reality. I had a great billet situation in Kingston with the Mullers, and they were like a second family to me. My apartment had its own entrance and it had a bedroom, shower, and kitchen. I didn't know how to cook, so the kitchen was used primarily for toasting bagels. One night, I was hanging out in the apartment with a couple of guys on the team. We drank some adult beverages, had some laughs, and then decided to go out because, as always, we were extremely bored.

Our team had a paintball outing planned for later in the week, and one of the guys wanted to make sure he had the biggest gun for the event, so he borrowed a $300 professional paintball gun from his buddy. We were driving in his pickup truck, looking for something to do around Kingston, when I noticed that the paintball gun had made its way to the back of the truck where three of us were sitting. One of the guys beside me started aiming and shooting paintballs at poles, walls, mailboxes, and anything else he could hit. His confidence started to grow, and he took a shot 30 feet behind a jogger, startling the runner and raising my blood pressure. We were immature and had no idea what we were doing. What else were 17-year-old boys living on their own going to do on a Tuesday night? As we continued down the road, we passed a biker leaning on his bike on the side of the road. My teammate continued to shoot at poles and as we drove by, I noticed the biker urgently making a call on what seemed to be a radio. He did not look happy — actually, he looked a lot like a police officer. And he was.

We hit the gas and turned into a nearby subdivision. Our truck turned left, it turned right, it turned left again, and then we made a final right onto an unknown street. There was a giant pine tree on the front lawn of the house, and I jumped out of the truck and threw the gun under the tree. I remember this like it was yesterday. We decided this was a good idea, just in case we got pulled over later in the evening and they searched the vehicle for the gun. We drove back to my billets' house, laughing the whole way, and sat down to watch some more TV. Two hours later, my buddy said, "That was a pretty expensive gun. Are we all going to chip in to replace it? My friend will not be happy if he finds out that we lost a three-hundred-dollar gun." We all agreed that we should go back for the gun. After all, we were making only $45 a week in salary, and that was barely enough for gas and a movie. The four of us headed out to my car because being the criminal masterminds that we were, we thought a car switch would thwart the authorities. It took us 45 minutes to find the same house, but we recognized the giant tree in the front yard. One of the guys walked onto the lawn and started crawling around under the tree. He yelled back to us, "It's not here!" That's when the neighbourhood lit up.

A police car came flying down the street with its lights flashing. We were busted. One of the guys took off sprinting down the street, removing his shirt in the process. I have no idea why he took his shirt off, but nothing we did really made any sense. A second player jumped into some nearby hedges and hid. What did I do, the genius mastermind? I slowly reclined my seat because the cop would never think to look in the Ford Tempo. The fourth player just stood there calmly, smiling. When the police car stopped, the officer came out slowly and said, "Tell the guy in the hedges to come out." He then flashed his light into the car, shook his head in disappointment, and told me to come out next. After five minutes of questioning, the shirtless player returned to the scene as well. The officer was surprisingly friendly, and he asked us to jump back into my car and follow him to the police station. It looked like our night was going to turn out okay after all. Things always had a way of working out for us, so it seemed.

We tried to get our story straight in the car, and we agreed we would tell the truth. When we walked into the station, there was a red-faced police officer dressed in short shorts and a sweat-soaked police shirt waiting for us.

To say he was not happy is an understatement. He came at us very quickly, yelling: "I have been looking for you guys all night. I have been riding my bike all around town." One of the guys began to snicker and said, "You were chasing us around town on a bicycle?" That was when things began to go sideways. We were all interviewed over the course of two hours, and the nice cop eventually told us to go home and get some sleep. We thought the incident was over, but we severely underestimated the bicycle cop.

My alarm went off the next morning, tuned to the local news station. After a brief commercial, I heard "Four Kingston Frontenacs were charged with assault with a deadly weapon last night." If you ever want to wake up quickly, have someone announce on the radio that you have been charged with a crime. Apparently, after we left the police station the night before, a local news reporter went to the station, as he did every night, to review the day's cases and write stories about events that people would want to know about. He came upon our case and recognized our names. The angry officer pressed to pursue the charges and the reporter found out before anyone could change his mind. Life lesson number one: never trust an adult on a bicycle. We were screwed. I got dressed and slowly headed upstairs to have breakfast, trying to clear my head. My billet always had fresh muffins and the newspaper ready for me in the morning. When I got upstairs, the newspaper was gone. I asked her if her husband had the paper, and she said they didn't deliver one that day. I eventually found the paper after breakfast, and I wish I had been better prepared for what it said. On the cover was a picture of the four of us, and the headline, "Four Frontenacs Charged with Assault with a Deadly Weapon." I told you that being called a prima donna earlier in the year wasn't half bad. If I had a shovel, I would have dug a hole and hid in it for a week.

We were called to the rink from school and we had to meet with our coach and the owner, Wren Blair. Wren was a legend in hockey and his claim to fame was finding Bobby Orr. He wasn't around often, but he luckily found the time to meet us that day. Wren seemed to be 100 years old, and we didn't have a clue as to what he was going to say. He proceeded to tell us a 30-minute story about the '60s, Bobby Orr, and the time his dad made him shine a crystal ball. He shined it, shined it, shined it, and when his dad said that it wasn't shiny enough, he shined it some more. I wanted to turn myself in for jail time rather than listen to any more of his stories.

The cherry on top of the sundae came four days later. On the front page of the *Kingston Whig-Standard* was a picture of a couple clutching their one-year-old baby. The headline? "They Shot at our Baby." (This bumped the Prima Donna headline to the third-worst headline about me in 1996.) It was a total lie, but we were toast. The truth was that one of the guys had shot at a sign 10 metres behind a man carrying a laundry basket. He had just left the laundromat and we had startled him, and it made him walk a little bit faster. About 80 metres ahead of him was a woman pushing a baby stroller. I remember it clearly because when I saw her and the stroller I thought, *Let's not do anything stupid.* The couple claimed that they were walking together at the time and we had shot at them. They claimed to have had an emotional time dealing with the situation ever since. After our lawyer did a little digging, we learned that the couple had a bit of trouble staying employed. They were currently collecting welfare, and they thought we were their big ticket to riches. They were slightly mistaken, as our combined salary was less than $200 a week. After all of the chaos, we were each ordered to do 200 hours of community service — we never hit anyone, we never had any intent to hit anyone, and we were really just four idiots ruining our careers. More importantly, people now thought I was a baby assassin.

The next couple of weeks were a complete nightmare, but I deserved it. We would do community service during the day between classes, go to practice at 4 p.m., and then have more community service at night. We attended minor hockey practices, served cookies at Red Cross blood banks, and worked too many smoke-filled bingo halls. We also helped out at local public schools and the Kingston Food Bank. I had volunteered for years with the Kingston Boys and Girls Club on my own time, but after the charge, they deemed me unsafe to work with kids. My first night at the smoky bingo, I was short $75 in my float. I had never been to a bingo before and these people were something to behold. Business was booming when the government cheques came in. Customers had mascots, trinkets, and good luck charms spread everywhere in their personal space, and if you touched one of their trinkets, you got the look of death. The players would call us over and order a Jackpot, a Super Jackpot, a Super Duper Jackpot, and any other random board they could buy. They would request ridiculous things like an even number board higher than the number five, and they had to touch it three times before the game started. In all of the confusion, I started charging the wrong amounts. The manager was pissed. He accused me of stealing and kicked me out.

Hockey continued to be brutal and the fans hated me. A common expression was, "Hey, Davis, if you aren't going to hit him, shoot him with your paintball gun!" Great folks. It was time for me to get out of Kingston, and quickly. My brother should've been banned from the Kingston arena because he spent half of his time at the game telling people to shut up while staring them down. He always had my back. It was something that an 18-year-old should never have to go through, but it helped me build resilience. And I would need it.

Every year, we took a tour of the Kingston Penitentiary. It was a maximum security prison at the time and it held the country's hardest and most dangerous criminals. Our assistant captain, Jason Sands, had a relative who worked as a supervisor at the penitentiary. He organized the tour for the team, and it was an opportunity for us to see the conditions in the prison and to scare us into making good decisions. To say the timing of the tour was terrible would be putting it lightly. The four of us from the paintball incident were still in the process of our court case, and it was still very public at the time. As we walked the penitentiary hallways, an inmate yelled, "Hey, Davis, we'll see you soon!" He mentioned the other guys by name as well, but all I could hear was mine as a giant shiver ran down my spine. I was too soft for prison.

The Kingston Pen was extremely creepy: every 20 steps, a giant steel door would slam shut behind you. We were within 30 feet of Paul Bernardo and the most dangerous criminals in Canada. We felt vulnerable the entire time. As we left one of the work rooms, the guards locked the door behind us, and we proceeded into the next room. We took five steps into the new room and an inmate came charging at us out of nowhere, with a mailbag over his head. Everyone screamed and started running in every direction. I hugged the guy next to me tightly. The inmate stopped immediately and took the mailbag off of his head. It was Jason Sands. One of the guards had locked him in there two minutes earlier to set up the prank. After catching my breath, I needed to change my underwear.

The trade deadline was January 10, just as it is now. I wanted out of Kingston, but I never requested a trade from the general manager. A trade request seemed like quitting, but I silently hoped it would come. My wish was granted. I was traded for two players and a couple of draft picks to the Sault Ste. Marie Greyhounds. They had a great team at the time, and they were making a run for the Memorial Cup. Joe Thornton had just returned from the World Junior team, and they were loading up for the playoffs. I couldn't wait to get there and escape my soiled reputation in Kingston.

People assume that when an OHL trade takes place, everyone's waiting, willing, and ready to go. It's not actually like that. Even though I wanted to get traded, I was still very comfortable in Kingston. We had a good team, I had great billets, and even though the general public disliked me, I still had some great friends. I really struggle with the idea of a no-trade clause. In my mind, it puts the player at a disadvantage because if the team tries to trade a player and the player says no, they're now on a team that doesn't want them. If your boss at work said you were fired, but you said you had a no-firing clause in your contract, would you still want to work there? It also gives the player too much power, and it restricts movement in the league. I think my bitterness with the no-trade clause comes from the entitlement that the new generation of players have. We were always on pins and needles, and if we got traded, we went without argument. Now players say, "I'm not going to Flint," or "I don't like the coach in Windsor, so I'm not going." It's weird to see a 17-year-old with so much power and control. Do you think the Soo was my first choice, eight hours away from my friends and family? Of course not, but it built character.

But I could be wrong. Without a no-trade clause, you were treated like a piece of meat. I went to school the day I was traded, and it was business as usual. There was a knock on the door of my math class, and the teacher asked me to come outside. When I stepped into the hall, I was met by an assistant coach and he told me that I needed to go to the rink as soon as possible. I drove my car to the Kingston Memorial Centre and walked into the GM's office. "We've traded you to the Soo. It's the best thing for you, and we appreciate all that you have done for us."

Within five hours, I was skating in warm-up at the old London Gardens in a Soo Greyhound jersey. My last name was safety-pinned on the back of my jersey during warm-up until somebody in the organization said it looked terrible. The equipment guy quickly removed the pins and sewed it on the jersey, and life was good. I played the game and when it was finished, I was on the bus headed to beautiful Sault Ste. Marie, Ontario. I can vividly remember crossing the Mackinac Bridge at 4 a.m. and wondering what the heck had happened to me. Earlier that morning, I had woken up at my billets', ate breakfast, and went to school. Now I was headed for the Soo on a bus with complete strangers, and I had no idea where I was sleeping that night. A teammate dropped me off at my new billets' house at 5 a.m. I had been told earlier that my room was in the basement. Have you ever wandered into a complete stranger's house at 5 a.m. and tried to find the room you would be living in for the next three months? I woke up three hours later, met my new family, and headed to Bawating Secondary School. I guess if you're building a case for having a no-trade clause, this would help your argument. I just think that there is a way of looking out for a player's best interests without giving him all of the power. Unfortunately, this comes with the assumption that the organization actually cares about the player.

The OHL emphasizes their commitment to education, but some of their decisions make you wonder. We were allowed to take a maximum of three classes because practice started at 3 p.m. Then, when you got traded, the courses didn't always match up between schools and the teachers weren't always teaching the same units. It was absolute chaos, and you did everything you could just to get all of your credits. Marks became secondary to just graduating high school. In Kingston, I was put into a Grade 12 English as a Second Language (ESL) class because the regular class was full. There were three of us on the team in the class, along with students from Spain, Bosnia, Croatia, and the Philippines. The teacher realized early on that we were "special exceptions," so our job was to make Earl Grey tea for the rest of the class and serve everyone steeped tea in Royal Doulton china. One day, our specific assignment was to take a stray cat that the teacher had found in her backyard to the local SPCA. We received 100 percent on that test. When it came time for the actual exam, we circled the adjectives, verbs, and pronouns and ended up with some pretty high marks.

When the OHL season was over, it was the exact same process. We returned to our hometown in late March or early April and hoped that our home school would allow us to register. All of the units were completely messed up, and I ended up missing huge chunks of the courses I took. The team didn't care about the chaos; they just wanted us out of their city as quickly as possible, before anything stupid happened. (You don't want four idiots driving around town with a paintball gun.) The league is trying to change this: it is very important in recruiting players away from the NCAA.

My first real school issue occurred after my trade from Kingston. I was at Bawating Secondary School for a total of two months, and I accomplished absolutely nothing. None of the courses matched up, and I slept in class most of the time. I returned home as soon as the playoffs were over and registered at my hometown school, Waterdown District High School. That's the reason I took the same math class three times in three years before I eventually passed. I first took Grade 11 math in Kingston and fell behind during hockey playoffs. When I returned home to finish the course, it was being taught in the reverse order and I had done most of the stuff already in Kingston, so I stopped attending. Apparently, it was not a great strategy and I received a 45 percent. I took the course the next year and skipped most of the class because I had taken it already and I thought I would pass the course easily. After all, I knew 45 percent of the material already. Well, I was traded, got completely screwed around in the Soo, and ended up receiving 40 percent when I returned back to Waterdown. I was getting dumber. The third time I took Grade 11 math, I finally got the credit.

So after taking the same course three times in three different high schools, in three different cities, I eventually passed. Most of my teachers were not very accommodating. We were treated as a nuisance and as make-work projects. One teacher in Waterdown deducted 20 percent on my final exam because I missed the test for the NHL Draft in St. Louis. Apparently, not everyone likes hockey. Teams now reluctantly allow players to stay in the city after the season is over, but online courses make the process much easier than before. I still hate math.

We had a very good team in the Soo, led by "Jumbo" Joe Thornton. He was 16 at the time, and he was an absolute stud. Joe was big, he was a great skater, he was the best passer I had ever seen, and he was tough. Joe doesn't get enough credit for his toughness, but he can fight anyone and he can get angry in a flash. We hit it off very quickly, as we had the same personalities and interests. Joe was a 10-year-old boy trapped in a 30-year-old's body. He was all about having fun and he loved to laugh. We sat together on the bus for most road trips, and he would do anything to pass the time. I remember him pulling individual hairs from his long mane and placing them on the faces of sleeping players to see if they would wake up. This would kill at least 30 minutes of boredom. Joe and I ended up travelling to Texas after the season to visit his brother who was teaching in the area. I can still remember going to see a Silverchair concert in Galveston, and Joe was absolutely destroying complete strangers in the mosh pit. His brother Alex had to go into the chaos and pull Joe out before something bad happened. We both knew Joe wasn't the one at risk of getting hurt. Joe was eventually going to be the number one pick in the NHL Draft, so his brothers were his bodyguards and his protection. We rode jet skis, put lemon juice in our hair to sun it blonde, and had a lot of good laughs.

His family was tight, and if you messed with Joe, you had to answer to the entire clan. I loved that about them. His brother Alex was a great guy, and he even hosted my brother at his place years later on a Boston trip. His other brother, John, became a lawyer and represented Joe with his own agency. He always talked about his parents, Wayne and Mary, and he loved being home in St. Thomas. Joe was one of the guys you were happy for when he made it to the NHL and you wished him all of the success he would eventually achieve. During my season in the Soo, his regular right winger got hurt one game and they put me on Joe's line. This was an attempt to get me out of my terrible slump, as he could make anyone look great. After two periods, a frustrated Joe asked the coach for anyone other than me on the right side. (I don't blame him.)

We lost touch over the years because when someone is making millions, it becomes awkward when you are a thousandaire. Five years ago, my son and I were in Pittsburgh to watch a game, and I saw Joe after the San Jose Sharks' practice. He went out of his way to talk to us for five minutes and set my son up with a 15-minute conversation with Brent Burns. He didn't have to do that, but it is a moment my son will never forget. He was one of the bright spots in my time in the Soo.

I continued to struggle after the trade, and I was miserable. Bus rides were consistently eight hours long and the travel took its toll on me. I had to double up seats every road trip because we had a veteran team. I could never sleep on the bus, so I was always tired. Don't get me wrong, we never had it as bad as the Western League or eastern teams in the QMJHL. Some teams in the Western League still have 18-hour road trips, and I can't even imagine the toll that those trips can take on your body. Curfew was 11 p.m. every night, and if you missed it by a minute, a local fan would call the coach to report the violation. We went from practice to a sports psychologist to a video session to home. There wasn't any free time, and I absolutely hated hockey. If I had been playing well, things may have been much different. My only laughs were in the dressing room with the guys and playing squash at the local racquet club.

A special treat was when one of our parents would stay the weekend in a nice hotel and leave their room key for us to use the facilities. For some reason, the key to enter the building would work for weeks after their departure. We enjoyed the hotel swimming pool and hot tub like it was a team-issued spa. It was a slight reprieve from hockey and the simplicity of our lives.

The billet house I lived in was awful. I lived in the basement and there was only one TV room. The couple argued non-stop and the arguments were loud. The dad was constantly yelling at the step-son and it was extremely awkward. They were huge hockey fans, and the dad always wanted me to watch the Leafs game with him. Little did he know that I hated the Leafs, and watching hockey was worse than watching *Coronation Street* with my grandparents. I hated the game of hockey. There was never any food in the house and a pregame meal was a bonus. Have you ever tried to play a hockey game after eating Kraft Dinner and wieners? What about a peanut butter and jam sandwich? The only phone was in their main living room, so there was no privacy. It was like being held hostage and the kidnappers were supervising every phone call. One night I came home with a cough, and my billet made me cut up onions, put them into wool socks, and sleep with them on in order to clear my body. I kept the cough with the added bonus of the stench of onions on me for an entire day. I always felt sorry for the mother: she was a really nice lady, caught in what seemed to be an abusive situation with her son. It was sad, but why was a junior hockey player living there? I spent most nights in bed, listening to arguments and staring at the ceiling. *Surely,* I thought, *there must be a happy ending to my miserable story.*

Our team took a a prison tour that season as well. One Saturday morning, we travelled to a medium-security prison in Michigan. The inmates at this prison spent the entire winter building an outdoor rink on the prison grounds. It was a thing of beauty. The ice was like glass, and the boards and benches were made of snow. Only the inmates who had been serving the longest, some of them up to 20 years, were allowed to be on the rink building crew. It was a major reward for time served and good behaviour. The inmates treated this responsibility like gold. When we arrived at the prison, our team walked to the yard, where we were surrounded by inmates. At this prison, the inmates could move around freely all day. Every two hours a horn would sound, and they would return to their cells for roll call. After roll call, everyone could go back to what they were doing. So when we walked into the prison yard with our skates hanging on our sticks, every Greyhound, myself included, had the same thought: *Please don't slash my throat with my Bauer Supremes.* We walked quickly and with purpose.

When the game started, the entire prison came out to watch. We were playing inmates in hand-me-down equipment supplied by the team. The inmates were watching on the right side of the rink, and guess what? I played right wing. Of course I decided to grow my hair out that year, and I had a little flow coming out of the back of my helmet. Every time I skated down the wing, some of the inmates would catcall and yell sexually suggestive phrases. I was afraid for my physical safety in more ways than one. By the third period, I was spending most of my time on the left wing and my shifts were down to 20 seconds at the most. If there was an NHL scout in attendance, he would have said that I hustled more than ever and my head was on a swivel. It was a great opportunity, but much like the Kingston tour, it was a relief when we finally left the front gates.

My second major concussion happened in Michigan against the Plymouth Whalers. I took a pass on the half boards and made a tape-to-tape pass to my centreman. I started to skate up the ice. I took four steps, and after that I don't remember anything but my world going completely dark. Apparently, a Plymouth forward hit me extremely late from behind, and on my blind side. I was immediately unconscious, convulsing on the ice. My grandmother and my dad had made the drive to Plymouth and they told me later that they walked right down to the glass to see what was wrong. I wasn't responding to anything, and the trainers were getting agitated. As a dad with a son currently playing hockey, it's difficult to imagine the emotions that my family was feeling. The trainers rushed me to the

Plymouth dressing room to see a doctor, and that was when I regained consciousness. I can only remember looking up and seeing the trainer, a Plymouth team doctor, Peter DeBoer (the Plymouth coach), and my dad. I had no idea how I got there and why my head hurt so badly. The doctor asked me some questions, and I didn't remember a single thing about the incident. It was like someone had airlifted me to an alternate universe.

I walked back to our dressing room, slowly got undressed, and showered. I couldn't figure out why I would have to do this all by myself, why I wasn't in an ambulance, and why nobody seemed concerned. That would become much clearer later on. I managed to board the bus and I tried to maintain whatever focus I had. I felt terrible. Minutes after departure, I rushed into the bathroom and threw up for the next 10 minutes. The management team at the front of the bus seemed more bothered that I was inconveniencing them. They finally relented and took me to a Detroit hospital on the strong recommendation of the trainer. In the emergency room, the doctor took one look at me and sent me for an MRI of my head to see if there was any damage to my brain. The MRI found bleeding on the brain, and I was quickly rushed to the ICU. After being hooked up to multiple machines and an IV, I finally felt comfortable and tried to fall asleep.

In the morning, my mom showed up at the hospital, and she spent the next three days with me, sleeping in the chair next to the bed at night. She made sure I had the proper medical attention that I needed. My bed pan was changed every couple of hours, and I was not allowed to walk for two days. The staff was fantastic, and I was treated very well. It was great to have some company, and I will never forget the sacrifice my mom made for me. I was eventually discharged and I headed back home to Carlisle after a three-day stay.

So why would a team make a player walk back to the dressing room on his own and board the bus for a sixteen-hour ride back to the Soo? Why would a team be in such a rush to cross the border when I had been unconscious and convulsing one hour before? Let me tell you why. Hockey is filled with a lot of people with very little integrity and, above all, their personal interests in mind. You are literally just a number. I found out later that the general manager at that time didn't want to pay U.S. medical costs. He wanted to sneak me back into Canada for our free health care, with no concern for my personal well-being. The doctor at the hospital told me that I was lucky that I came in when I did. The brain bleed would have continued to swell, which is very dangerous.

But hey, let's save some money, right?

A couple of months later, the team sent my parents the $15,000 hospital bill. It included the three-day stay in ICU, two MRIs, and all the other health care that I had received. Let me repeat that. The team billed me for my own traumatic brain injury. My agent was furious and he argued with the team daily. The general manager was lying to my mom and lying to my agent at the same time, but thanks to my agent's hard work and after a long period of conflict, the team settled and paid my bill. I will always be thankful to Allan Walsh for his time and energy in protecting me and my family. It really felt great to know that the team I played for cared so much about my well-being and safety. Later in my career, when I was playing for the Ottawa 67's in the Memorial Cup, I saw the owners and the GM who tried to screw my family. It took everything within me to bite my lip and not say a word. I will never forget how I was treated by the Greyhounds, and it's a reminder of the importance of treating everyone with respect and integrity.

I flew back to the Soo for the first round of the playoffs and I was cleared to skate. Our coach at the time, Joe Paterson, showed up at the airport to pick me up. We had a great conversation on the way to my billets' house and he made me feel like I was wanted. Joe told me he thought that I could contribute to the team in the playoffs. He was a good man and he always treated me with respect, even though I played terribly for most of my time in the Soo. The coaching staff skated me hard after practice, trying to get me into game shape. I felt 90 percent for the first time in a long time. The team was eventually upset by the Guelph Storm in the second round, and I never got the chance to play again that season. Looking back on it, I'm thankful. It was a blessing for my future that I didn't take another hit at that time. I could finally go home and give myself eight full months to heal without contact.

You may be saying to yourself, this still sounds pretty good. You played in the OHL and you had the honour of getting drafted by the Washington Capitals — I would do anything for my son to have those opportunities. With the right break, anything could happen, and if this book ended right now, this could be considered a successful career. But I would disagree with you. What you don't understand is that the only thing I gained from this "success" was misery. I hated the game, I was embarrassed to walk around my town, my life was in a constant post-concussion fog, and I felt like I had let my family down. They had sacrificed a lot to give me every opportunity to succeed, and at that point I just wanted to walk away from the game. I protected my family from my true mental state by distancing myself and intentionally ignoring the circumstances of my reality.

My friends didn't have to work out every day; they could do whatever they wanted to do on the weekends, and I felt like I was missing out on everything. I was actually jealous of them. All that I wanted was to be a normal teenager without the expectations of my coaches, my agent, my parents, and, most of all, myself. I was having trouble looking at myself in the mirror. The little boy who lived to play hockey was long gone. So do you still want your child to play in the NHL?

CHAPTER 7
KILLER AND THE NATION'S CAPITAL
(1997–99)

After the season, our youth pastor John Latta told me that Muskoka Woods Sports Resort was looking for someone to help with their hockey program. I intended to head up north to help out for a week, but I ended up staying for the entire summer. It seemed to be a pattern that I was creating in my life, where I left for what was to be a short period of time but never came back. It was during my time up north at MWSR that I could actually clear my head. I realized that I had a purpose, and I could refocus on my life outside of hockey. I woke up each day overlooking Lake Rosseau, surrounded by people my age, living life to the fullest. There was something different about this place as people lived each day with the faith that there was more to life, a life with meaning and purpose beyond hockey. It was refreshing, and I felt like a new person. I can't quite remember how I spent most of my time during the seven weeks that the hockey camp wasn't running, but I do know I trained hard and prepared myself for NHL training camp and another year in the OHL. During my time at Muskoka Woods, I was asked to play in this "elite" ball hockey league in Burlington every Thursday, for a team of guys I didn't even know. I was the only non-Italian on the team, and I was their designated ringer. The team paid me $100 cash for gas and expenses per game, so of course I was in. One of the men who ran the hockey camp at MWSR, Bob Fukumoto, offered to drive me to Burlington and back for a game. Bob was the pastor, and he saw it as a time to share and provide me with some much needed mentorship. In the third period of the game, this player on the other team kept slashing my hands whenever I touched the ball. I couldn't take it anymore and I snapped. I took a vicious baseball swing with my stick at the opposing player and it started a brawl of epic proportions. I was banned from the ball hockey league for life, and Bob sat silently in disbelief during the car ride home. He couldn't believe what he had just seen, and it was an awkward three hours back to Muskoka Woods.

I left the camp and flew into Washington in early September. The training camp was uneventful, and I had an average performance with the team. I hadn't played hockey at that high of a level in over seven months, so it was a huge adjustment for me. The game felt like it was being played at three times the speed. During my time up north, it was very difficult to find an elite summer skate and the OHL training camp was not at NHL speed. My time away from the game as I dealt with my concussion affected my playing ability, and I was not prepared. The Capitals returned me to the Soo after four days of training camp, and I was prepared to make a difference in the OHL once again.

The Soo hired a new coach over the summer after Joe Paterson had left to become an assistant coach in the American Hockey League (AHL). It was immediately made clear that the new coach was not a fan of Justin Davis. I'll be honest — I wasn't exactly 100 percent yet, nor at full speed, but this coach was not a great human being at that time. I'm not sure if he was even a great hockey coach. If I had to choose one coach to *not* emulate in any way . . . it would be him. He had just come from the old Colonial

Hockey League and it was clear that his coaching style was a reflection of that league. If you weren't going to hit, be physical, or fight, this wasn't the place for you. I was a player who was the exact opposite of what he was looking for. I wanted to contribute offensively and be a responsible player in my own end of the rink. The coach wouldn't talk to me directly at any time, as positive communication would be seen as a sign of weakness. He didn't need to communicate verbally, as his actions, aggression, and attitude were more than clear. When you get into an altercation with one of your teenage players on a stationary bike in a junior hockey dressing room because you don't like his work ethic, the tone is set for the team. If a player in my position on the depth chart reported this altercation, they would be released. I was playing terribly, so I had no value to the team.

Coaches held all the cards and players were powerless. Mike Babcock and Bill Peters led from a position of power and fear in the NHL, and nobody said anything until very recently, when the zeitgeist shifted. Grown men playing in the greatest league in the world were held power-less by their coaches' tyranny. So you can understand why David Frost and Graham James had the opportunity to prey on vulnerable teenage players in junior hockey. Junior hockey coaches craved power, and we were their pawns to gain NHL employment. Even worse, who do you report this misconduct to when your coach is also the GM and he hired his own assis-tants? The Brian Kilreas, who stayed behind to make a positive difference in the CHL, were few and far between. I was just beginning to understand this part of the game and my role in the process.

In an exhibition game in Sudbury, things started to get physical late in the game. At that time, if you fought in the third period of an exhibition game, you got kicked out. For OHL veterans, it was a green light to hit the showers early and save yourself from playing more than you had to. I tried to prove to the new coach that I wasn't scared, and I ended up having a really good fight in the third period. After the game, he yelled at me for shortening the bench and he said nothing of my altercation. If I hadn't fought, he would have told me that I was scared. I realized then and there that this situation was not going to work. I was trying everything possible to gain his approval, but it was always to no avail. Although this coach went on to do some big things in hockey — even coached in the NHL — and is still coaching at a very high level, I hope he saw the faults in his ways and has adapted his communication style since. Hopefully, working with men allowed him to humanize people and lose his saviour complex. He may not have known it, but it was just a game and he wasn't God.

I am overcome with emotion as I write this, because deep down, I am still afraid of these people. I always tried to seek their approval, and the risk of the blowback I'll receive after exposing these frauds overwhelms me. This is what it must feel like to leave a cult. You become scared of the reaction of the people that treated you so poorly and you become terrified of the repercussions of telling the truth. I know that when people read this, their first reaction will be to demonize me as a person and be critical of my hockey ability. I know that and I am okay with it. I've consistently made mistakes in my personal life, and I know that I didn't make the NHL because I wasn't good enough. Criticizing me doesn't change what has happened to countless careers, and having this conversation will hopefully change the game for the better. Hockey has been hiding behind the hockey code for too long, and we were always told, *What happens in the room stays in the room*. Why did I want to protect the game so badly? I learned at 15 that it was normal to be shaved and to drink someone else's bodily fluids. I learned at 17 that someone could yank on a skate lace attached to my genitals as hard as they wanted to because my body belonged to the team. I watched my first pornographic movie on a team bus with players masturbating all around me. What was abnormal behaviour became routine. I was becoming a deviant and I didn't even realize it. Spit on my back in the shower? No problem. Piss all over me when I'm shampooing, that's hilarious. A rookie put shaving cream in your gloves? Go take a crap in his skates and stick around to watch his reaction.

I had no idea that the hockey code wasn't normal until I entered the real world and got a job. I thought that other people were the weird ones. I was a great kid with fantastic parents and I entered the real hockey world as a naive 13-year-old. It took me 20 years and three of my own kids to realize that the adults involved were the ones who failed me. I can remember sitting in my room in the basement of my billets' house in the Soo, sobbing, listening to the domestic abuse going on upstairs, and trying to forget about my failure and disappointments as a hockey player. I'd let down my parents, my coach, and everyone who ever believed in me. I did not have access to a phone in my room and I was deeply depressed; isolated in the basement. I wanted my life to end. I wanted to erase my pain, and I didn't want it to continue. Eliminating myself would end the throbbing headaches I was having every day after the numerous mismanaged concussions. Suicide might show the coach that he was wrong and he couldn't continue this way. My absence would allow others to see the good in my life and it would expose the broken world of junior hockey. So what saved me from this decision? I lived with another player at this time, Tim Zafiris, who showed up at the right time. My parents phoned every night, and most of all, I was sent home from the Soo before any more damage could be done. I am thankful that God actually had a plan for me.

I happily left the Soo in the middle of September. I drove home eight hours and waited for a trade. The Ford Tempo was replaced by a Ford Taurus and it was racking up the kilometres and getting a good tour of Ontario. Going home was the best thing for both parties involved. Even though I was there for only five months, I often say I spent two years in the Soo because that is what it felt like. I sucked, I was concussed, I was emotionally broken down, I was verbally abused, charged with a $15,000 medical bill, and quickly forgotten by everyone involved in the organization. If Washington wasted an 85th overall pick on me, then the Soo lost two players and multiple picks for absolutely nothing. There was a silver lining for Greyhound fans: I got a call from my agent a few days after returning home. The Ottawa 67's traded a sixth-round pick for my services, and the Soo recouped a draft pick after all. Allan told me that Brian Kilrea called him and said, "The kid scored every time we played him, so if he can do that here, I'll take him." I was pumped. Finally, someone knew me from watching me play in Kingston and he actually wanted me, warts and all. I made it to Ottawa that same day.

Killer. What can I say about a man who is in the Hockey Hall of Fame, who is the winningest junior coach of all time, who is the best coach I ever played for, and, most of all, is a great human being? I walked into the dressing room after practice the first day, and he came out of his office and shook my hand. Brian talked to me for 10 minutes and asked me about my drive. He went out of his way to introduce me to the guys, and he made me feel extremely comfortable from the very beginning. I talked to Brian more on my first day in Ottawa than I did with the coach of the Greyhounds in my entire two weeks there. On the tour of the dressing room, Killer walked into the training room and said, "That's the ice machine. It's to keep the beer cold. If you get injured, walk to the Zamboni room and take their ice." I knew I had hit the jackpot.

The team couldn't find me a billet right away so I got to live with the Kilreas for a couple of days. It was a surreal moment as I remembered sitting in the Cambridge dressing room three years ago watching Spud and Killer enjoy a cigar after a Junior B game, and now here I was playing for him. Brian drove me to his house where he had lived for over 40 years. His wife, Judy, greeted me at the door and told me dinner was ready. I sat with Killer and Judy for over an hour, eating dinner and talking about life. I felt human for the first time in a long time. Brian walked me to the basement after dinner and showed me where I would be sleeping. He told me I could have the basement for now and I could sit in his chair. On one side of the leather recliner was a table holding a phone and on the other side was a fridge filled with beer. The TV was 10 feet in front of the chair. Brian put an NHL game on for me and said to help myself to the beer fridge. He said I could make as many calls as I wanted and to let my family know that I was settled. For some reason, I felt compelled to watch the game and I actually enjoyed it. It was almost Pavlovian — it now seemed like I only enjoyed hockey when I was in a happy place. It had taken me over a year to find this place again, but I took a deep breath and couldn't stop smiling. I finally had a private place to call my parents, I had just eaten a home cooked meal, and I had a safe, quiet bed to sleep in. You would think this would be the norm for every junior hockey player, but it was not something I had experienced since the Mullers' house in Kingston. I tried to use my calling card to call my parents but Killer had an old rotary phone. By the time you circled one number around the dial and started the next one, the calling card would time out. I began to laugh as this was 1997, not 1962. Little did I know that this was the first story of thousands that I'd gather during my time with the Ottawa 67's and Brian Kilrea.

During one of my first weekends in Ottawa, my brother, Kyle, came to visit. My brother and sister are much older than me, so our relationships were very different. My sister always looked after me when I was younger and she spent a lot of time with me. We have some pretty good memories together and starting from a young age, she took me wherever she went. My buddies and I still laugh about the car that she used to drive — it had terrible brakes. She would drop us off at day camp, and we would jump out of the car while it moved at 10 kilometres per hour, as it attempted a rolling stop. My brother was in high school and I didn't spend as much time with him because I was so much younger. When I got older, we grew closer and he made numerous road trips to wherever I was playing. There was never any jealousy with Kyle, and he was always my protector when things went wrong. When I was 11, I was playing in a church league 3-on-3 hockey tournament with adults. I was one of the better players on the ice and some of the adults started hacking and slashing me every chance they got. At one point, I came back to the bench crying and my brother asked me what was wrong. Before I could finish the story, he had hopped the boards and was chasing two guys around the ice, eventually fighting both of them. Kyle was banned from the tournament.

Years later, when I was 18 years old and playing in the OHL at six foot four and 190 pounds, he hadn't changed. We were playing in another "fun" church league tournament in Toronto, and this guy kept slashing me to the point where I'd had enough. I turned around, tomahawk chopped him across the wrist, and dropped my gloves. Before I could do anything, my brother had jumped head-first over the boards, pulled the guy's jersey over his head, and was throwing continuous upper cuts to the guy's face. I yelled, "Kyle, stop, you're killing him!" After that, he was escorted from the ice. Later, I would try to explain to him that I was 18 years old now and I could probably handle myself.

So on Kyle's first trip to Ottawa, his patience was put to the test. We went out for dinner after the game and then headed out to the bar with the rest of the team. It was one of my first weekends as an Ottawa 67. We just wanted to go out, meet the guys, and have a little fun. My brother was always up for anything, so he settled in and was having a great time. Around midnight, there was a huge commotion on the dance floor. Punches were being thrown and a small brawl was breaking out in the middle of the pack. Out of nowhere, Kyle climbed onto the brass rail surrounding the dance floor, and he Jimmy "Superfly" Snuka'ed his way off the top rail into the crowd. It was a sight to behold and I can still picture it to this day. I was minding my own business at a table away from the chaos, but Kyle didn't know that. He was trying to find me to make sure I was safe and to get me out of any trouble. It was hilarious to watch because he was asking guys if they were on my team and then proceeding to fight guys who said they weren't. Both of us only knew half the team at this point, so he cleared house until he realized I was okay. We had a trainer in Ottawa who was too lazy to use the bathroom whenever he was out, so he would just pee under the table into an empty beer bottle. (Really.) I was sitting beside him during the fight, trying to protect him as some random guy was punching him as he relieved himself into a bottle of Coors Light under the table. After the commotion, we had some good laughs and returned home. All I could think was, *Here we go again. We are going to get in trouble as a team tomorrow when the coach finds out what happened last night.* But we never heard a word about it. In retrospect, Killer always knew what was going on but he also knew when to step in and always chose his spots wisely. This was junior hockey in Ottawa, and it was a whole new world for me.

Killer ran the same practice every day. I'm not kidding. It was the same drills, same order, every single day. The pace was fast and there wasn't any board instruction time to take a breather, as you knew the next drill anyway. Practice was only 45 minutes long, but you were always exhausted when it finished. It was all attacking off the rush with speed and regroups with flow. Killer would stand at centre ice for each drill with the pile of his pucks at his feet. Nobody else in hockey did this, as he was essentially a landmine in the middle of the centre ice area. Once in a while an errant puck would hit his pile of pucks at centre, sending the pucks everywhere. He would scream a little bit and tell you to wake up but it was nothing terrible. You got used to it the longer you played and learned to avoid his pile of pucks. If you wanted to see him get really angry, you just had to knock him over. Every two months some poor soul would clip him accidentally at the red line, and it was like watching a grandparent fall off the couch in slow motion. You would bite your lip so hard it would bleed, but you could not make eye contact with him or let him see you smile. He would regain his footing and scream at the perpetrator while giving him a death glare. His stare made the name "Killer" seem more than appropriate, and nobody had a better glare than Brian Kilrea. When you were new to the team, it took a while to realize that a 60-year-old man and a pile of pucks would be in the centre of the ice during a breakout and double regroup drill. Much like everything else in Ottawa, you got used to it.

Killer was one of the funniest coaches I have ever met, and his one-liners were legendary. I was working out in the weight room one day after practice, which also served as a trainer's room, his office, and the home of the hot tub. After a quick set on the bench press, Killer looked at me and said, "Hey, Davis, I've been here forty years and do you know how many times I've seen someone score from the weight room?" I said, "No, how many?" "None, get dressed and go home!"

Another time, one of our players, Dan Tessier, arrived at practice with only five minutes left before going on the ice. He was rushing to his stall and Killer walked into the room. He looked at him and said, "Hey, Tessier, you have four minutes. If I get dressed before you do and make it to the ice, the entire team skates." Dan rushed into his underwear and started to get his stuff on. Killer came around the corner a minute later and he was wearing his skates, a whistle, his 67's hat, and his hockey gloves, and was holding a stick. He was wearing nothing else. Just a completely naked 60-year-old man, laughing his ass off, saying, "I beat you, Tessier. Now we skate." He went back into his office and got dressed, but it brought the house down with laughter.

Killer was brutal on goalies. "Just stop the puck" was the extent of his instruction. One of our goalies let in a terrible shot from the red line to lose a game, and he snapped. He stormed into the dressing room and yelled, "We would have had the two points if Hillier could stop a curling rock from centre ice!" The next day he had the entire team line up across the red line with five pucks each. One by one, down the line, we would shoot from the red line, trying to score on him. We did this for ten minutes while Killer yelled, "Now you can stop it. Eh, Hillier?!" It was his way of teaching someone a lesson, but the guys found it hysterical and were trying to bounce pucks in. We really wanted to score. The goalies never really found it amusing, but I don't remember anyone scoring from centre again. Killer did stuff like this all the time. When he thought a rookie forward's hands were too high on his stick, he would tape his gloves to the stick in the correct position. The kid had to practice with his hands attached to his stick and when he went for water, he'd rest the glove and stick combo on the boards. At a different skate, one of the other first-year players accidentally hit Killer at centre on a regroup drill. After Killer got back onto his feet, he benched the player for the rest of practice. When it was his turn to do the next drill, everyone else had to sit on the bench. Killer told him this was so "he wouldn't hurt any of the regulars." The poor guy had to break out, regroup, and attack 3-on-2 all by himself while everyone else sat on the bench and laughed.

The guys loved him, respected him, and treated him like their own dad. In between periods, Killer would erupt on a mistake somebody made. We were very good both of the years I played in Ottawa, going 40-16-9-1 in 1998 and losing to the Guelph Storm in the finals. My second year we went 48-13-7 and won the Memorial Cup. We didn't lose often, but when we did, we knew we were in for it. He would enter the locker room five minutes after the period ended and would pace around with his head down. You would always stare at the floor in front of your stall, afraid to make eye contact because that would remind him of the terrible play that you had made earlier. Once you locked eyes, he would look at you and scream until his face turned red. He'd storm out of the dressing room and we would all make fun of the guy he'd just ripped on, laugh, go get a drink, or tape our sticks. You ended up with extremely thick skin and you never took anything he said personally. What I loved about him is that he could tell you that you had made the worst pass he'd seen in 30 years and that he should trade you. Then the game would end and he'd pass you in the hallway, ask about your family and make sure everything was all right at your billets' house. He'd tell you to have a great night, to not get into any trouble, and sometimes he'd give you $20 for gas. He completely separated on-ice from off-ice, and Killer never held a grudge. He would only make a trade if you requested one, so everyone knew they were staying put in Ottawa and there wasn't a threat of getting traded. He yelled at you because he knew you were one of his own and he was going to make you better. Too many times organizations give up on guys because it's easier to trade them away than spend the time to develop them. Killer believed if he drafted you or traded for you, it was up to him to make you a better hockey player. It was such a different concept than what I had experienced before, and it made me extremely loyal to the man.

On every road trip, Killer travelled with his three best friends. He had known two of them since high school and they grew up together in the city of Ottawa. Their names were Tank and Stumpy. Tank was a huge man and he always sat behind Killer on the bus. Tank's claim to fame was that he could drink a case of beer between Ottawa and any city in the league that was two or more hours away. He didn't drink his beer, he swallowed it. It was a sight to behold and he would pace himself based on the location of the bus from our home arena. One day we were coming back from Belleville, and Tank was sitting with our radio commentator, Dave Schreiber. Dave was a talented broadcaster who was a veteran of the business. When the bus pulled out of Belleville onto the 401, Tank asked Dave if he wanted a beer. Dave said, "Sure, why not?" When Dave was done with his drink, Tank asked if he wanted another beer and Dave said, "That's okay, one beer was just fine." The bus pulled into the Ottawa Civic Centre three hours later and Killer asked Tank where the rest of the case went. He said, "Tank, you didn't drink twenty-four beers on the way from Belleville, did you?" Tank responded, "No, Brian, Schreibs and I split it."

Tank had two jobs on each road trip. The first job was to get off the bus on the way to the game, go into the Beer Store, buy the beer, and pack the coolers tight with ice. His second job was to hand out game socks to each player in the dressing room. Tank's first job was obviously the most important, and it led to us being late for two to three games a year. I remember one year we had a road game in Peterborough. We experienced bad traffic on the highway and we were running 10 minutes late for warm-up. As we entered the city, the bus made its usual turn into the Beer Store. Tank strolled off the bus and returned carrying the cases of beer without a care in the world. The game could wait. We walked into the Peterborough Memorial Centre with our bags, trying to avoid the sold out crowd standing around the concourse area. There was an announcement on the PA, "Due to bad traffic, the Ottawa 67's have arrived late and the game will be delayed twenty minutes." It wasn't the traffic that was the issue, it was Tank packing the coolers in the middle of the Beer Store parking lot that caused the delay.

Stumpy had just one job: jersey distribution. He would walk around the dressing room before the game and hand you your jersey. After that, his work was done. Stumpy was five foot five, looked 70 years old, and was the strongest man I had ever met. His handshake or pinching of your neck would bring you to your knees. Rumour had it that he was the toughest man in Ottawa in his twenties, and he would fight anyone who tried him on a Friday night. Killer and Stumpy would tell epic stories of his clashes. I think if I tried to fight 70-year-old Stumpy, I would have survived for as long as I could run away from him. Stumpy would sit across from Killer on the bus and one seat back. He would drink his rye, pass out, and we would watch the lit cigarette in his mouth get closer to burning his lips while he slept. We would set a timer and take bets on how long it would take for the burning ash to reach his mouth before it woke him up.

The last man in the crew was Killer's assistant, Bert. Bert had been with Killer since they coached minor hockey together and he was also his golfing partner. I'm not sure that Bert knew how to skate, as he sat in the stands each practice and would often fall asleep. In between drills, we would shoot pucks at Bert just to see if we could wake him up. I think he came to practice to say he was there, and so he could have two or three drinks and a cigar with Brian. He smoked a cigar every day, wherever he wanted. On our bus trips, Killer and Bert would smoke cigars and Stumpy would smoke cigarettes. We had to have a special driver who didn't care about the smoking, so we found a guy who smoked while he drove, too. Basically, we travelled in a giant hot box. There was a latch at the back of the bus that opened a small air vent, creating a tiny space for air to get in. It was mandatory that we always kept it open. We opened the bathroom window as well so we could get as much clean air as possible into our lungs. It was cold, but it beat the clouds of smoke wafting to the back of the bus. When you got off the bus to get your bag, it was like a nightclub letting out at 1 a.m. Everyone smelled like smoke and felt terrible.

A couple of years later, the same driver was driving the team on a road trip. Everyone was up to their old tricks and the bus was filled with smoke as usual. The driver was minding his own business with a cigarette in his mouth, when he suddenly passed out. It caused the bus to veer towards a nearby ditch. Killer, sitting in the front seat, leapt into the driver's chair and steered the bus to safety. When a reporter asked how Killer reacted so quickly, he said, "On this bus, if there is only one beer left, you have to be quick."

On the hockey side of things, everything was going well. I was starting to score again, and we were encouraged to play with skill and creativity. There weren't any systems to suffocate you, and it was nice not to feel confined when you played the game. I was playing on the third line with two really good players, and I couldn't care less that I wasn't on the top unit. Killer played three lines equally and barely played his rookies. You earned your ice time and it was a rite of passage in Ottawa. My left winger was Lance Galbraith and he was the toughest player pound for pound that I ever played with. He was five foot ten and 165 pounds soaking wet, and he would fight anyone. At 15 years old, Lance was in trouble for stealing cars and was likely headed to juvenile detention. Brain Kilrea wrote a letter to the judge saying he'd take care of him if he was allowed to come to Ottawa. The judge allowed Killer to take care of Lance, and he became the most popular Ottawa 67 ever. One night when we were in Oshawa, the Generals had a new van with a picture of their goalie saving a shot from Lance on the side of it. Killer called him to the front of the bus and said, "Lance, you're famous, you made the side of the Generals team van." Lance replied, "Can

you believe it? I used to steal those things and now I'm on the side of one."
I loved playing with Lance, and we had a lot of success together. He would
go on to play professional hockey for a long time afterwards and end up
winning two Kelly Cups in the East Coast Hockey League (ECHL) after
winning a Memorial Cup with us in Ottawa. Lance racked up over three
thousand penalty minutes in his career, and he was a great teammate everywhere he played. It would be tough to find a player who played with more
heart. Tragically, Lance passed away in a car accident at the age of 42, and
it was a gut punch to all of his former teammates, coaches, and friends. We
always thought Lance was indestructible. He will never be forgotten.

Two weeks into my time in Ottawa I received a huge break. Literally.
The import player Petr Mika from the Czech Republic broke his wrist (or
technically, he had it broken: in practice one day, he took a slap shot that hit
our goalie in the head; the goalie immediately chased him into the corner
and two-handed him across the wrist). As a result, I was moved to the top
line and I never looked back. I ended up scoring 32 goals that season and had
my best OHL campaign. Troy Stonier was my centreman and he was amazing. I think I scored 15 tap-in goals on odd-man breaks that season, along
with the usual five off of my pants. When you look back on your career and
the things that didn't go your way, it's important to see the breaks that did.
My time in the Soo prepared me for this success, and I was grateful for the
new opportunity. It built resilience and strength in me that was vital for my
future. If those bad things had never happened to me, I wouldn't have been
able to fully enjoy the good things that eventually did happen.

My billets were really nice people, but it was a strange situation. The lady
was a nurse and she was extremely friendly. When she wasn't on the night
shift, she would cook a great dinner and I enjoyed her company. The dad was
a piece of work. He woke up every day at 5 a.m. and wandered downstairs in
his housecoat to have a Pepsi and a smoke. It became an interior alarm clock
for me as the second-hand smoke seeped under my door. He would start
making phone calls at 6:30 a.m. in a booming voice, not worried in the least
that anyone was still sleeping. He didn't have a job, so I have no clue who he
was calling or why he had to get up that early. He was on disability due to

a back injury but drove a brand new black Suburban with tinted windows and would somehow be able to build a dock for his Quebec cottage in our driveway. My mom would call the house, and he would answer every time the phone rang. When she would ask if I was home, he would say, "I'll get the slutbag." I was thrilled, obviously. He did the same when my girlfriend called. I spent a good deal of time trying to explain to people that I had no idea why he called me that. I built a clothing rack in my car and hung it across the back seat. To avoid my clothes smelling like smoke, I would keep my wardrobe in the car and keep only pajamas or dirty clothes in my room. I was spending half of my life trying to avoid second-hand smoke and keep my clothes smelling fresh. I also placed a towel across the bottom of my door to keep the smoke from coming in.

Halfway through the season, I took a brutal crosscheck across my ribcage. It was so painful to breathe after the injury and the thought of coughing or laughing brought me to tears. I had the team doctor look at it, but he said it looked fine. By "team doctor," I mean veterinarian. Killer had a buddy who was a doctor, but the rumour was that he was actually a vet. Either way, he was our designated team doctor and I was expected to listen to him. Every time he came into the dressing room, the guys would make animal sounds after he walked through. The team gave me a flak jacket from the Ottawa Roughriders that their quarterback used to wear, and it was strapped on tightly to protect me during games and practices. I even wrapped some foam on top of the jacket just to be safe, as any contact was painful. After two weeks, the pain continued to worsen and I could hardly breathe without wincing. I told Killer my ribs were throbbing and he responded, "I had a guy here twenty years ago who thought he broke his ankle. He wanted to take his skate off, and I told him not to do it. He slept through the night with the skate on and scored three goals the next day. He didn't take the skate off the next night and he scored another three goals. After that game he took his skate off and it turned out he had a broken ankle. But guess what? He had six more goals." What does that even mean?

I guess the point was that if I found out that I actually had broken a rib, then I wouldn't have got those points in my last five games. My thinking was,

If my ribs are broken, I'd rather they not puncture a lung or pierce an internal organ. Just being a little selfish I guess. My billet got me into the emergency room quickly, as she was working that night, and the doctor saw me and sent me for x-rays. When the x-rays came back, he said, "Well, there's good news and bad news. The bad news is two ribs are broken, but the good news is that the round calcium ball on your ribs means that they are healing because they've been broken for three weeks." I came to practice the next day and told Killer I was going to be out for a little bit. He responded, "I played with a guy in the AHL who got so drunk he fell off the balcony of the hotel and hurt himself badly. We didn't want the coach to know so we dressed him and sent him out to warm-up and pretended he got hurt in the warm-up." So what was his point on that one? I think you know where this is going. Then he finished with, "I played for Eddie Shore and I had three broken ribs one year and you know what? I still had to play!" Tough to argue with that.

I knew deep down that if I said I couldn't play, Killer would respect my decision. Part of Brian's aura was his connection to "old time hockey," but I always inherently believed that he knew it was wrong. When I had a groin injury earlier in the season, I sat out two games and he gave me the latitude to decide when I was healthy to return. This was the contradiction of Killer: the gruff, screaming hockey legend who valued the traditions of the game versus the father figure who protected his players. The ball was always in the players' court and this internal reasoning made players grow up quickly. The Eddie Shore farce was a subliminal technique to make sure you were really injured versus just being "hurt." Of course, my interpretation comes from the trust and adoration I had for him as a coach, and I understand others may view it differently.

The guys on the team were great, and it was one of the best dressing rooms I've ever been a part of. Most days after practice we would sit in our half equipment for hours and talk. Nobody was ever in a rush to go home. We never had curfew and we were always accountable to our teammates and to ourselves. Killer's thinking was that you could stay out until 2 a.m. and do whatever you wanted — but if it affected how you played the game, you were going to hear about it. Every Saturday morning after a Friday night win, eight guys would show up in their suits from the night before. Killer wasn't stupid and we always skated it out in the first 30 minutes. I loved being able to go to the movies any time I wanted to or slide over to the Hull casino and not be worried about curfew. We were treated like men until we acted like boys. Once in a while we would lose, and Killer would yell that he's calling curfew at midnight. We all knew he'd make two phone calls and realize it was too much work.

As a result of this responsibility that was given to us, we never initiated the rookies. Killer wouldn't allow it. The rookies sat two players to a seat, they loaded the bus, and they picked up pucks after warm-up. Nobody treated them much differently and rookies were not humiliated at any time. Killer created his own hierarchy in the initiation system by making the rookies earn their playing time and by treating them like it was their first year. You knew that as you got older, he would give you more responsibility and playing time. If Killer got mad after a road loss, he would yell, "Everyone on the bus in twenty minutes or we leave without you. And all the veterans get one beer tonight." Apparently, limiting you to only one beer on the bus was what he considered punishment.

School was going great and I was actually engaged and keeping up. We had a school liaison with the team named Ms. Kelly. She was an amazing woman and the guys treated her like gold. Every Tuesday she would bake cookies and bring them in for the team. She knew we wouldn't pass up free food, and by doing so, she was getting us into a room to find out what assignments we were missing and what issues we might be having at school. She understood early on that I was a smart kid who was just not that interested in school. She placed me into courses she thought I would like, with really good teachers, and I took off academically. I was able to get the prerequisites I needed for university, and I am forever thankful for all that she did for me. It shouldn't take seven years to graduate high school but everyone works at their own pace, right? We went to a great school and our teachers and the students all liked us. That was a rarity in the league. Teachers would come to our games and we would get them tickets whenever we could. Years later, I made it onto the Wall of Fame at Canterbury High School.

My second year in Ottawa was the best hockey year of my life. I was in my overage year and I lived with another overage player, Dan Tudin, in our very own house. OHL teams are allowed to begin the season with three over-age 20-year-olds on their roster. These players are highly valued as they provide leadership and experience to the young players on the team. It was a privilege to be one of these designated players in my last OHL season. Jeff Hunt had just bought the team and he was an amazing owner. In one year, he had doubled attendance and put in a bid for the Memorial Cup — he was passionate about the team. Jeff asked Dan and me to house-sit his dad's home when he went to Florida for the winter. It was an offer we couldn't refuse. We lived on our own, collected billet money, and did whatever we wanted day after day.

A typical day as an over-ager in Ottawa was pretty simple. I would wake up at 8 a.m., get dressed, and head to Killer's house to pick up the team van. He always left the keys in the mailbox, and I would leave my car parked on the road. I would hop into his van that was covered in 67's wrap and immediately pop out whatever CD he had in the stereo. Killer loved Anne Murray and Nana Mouskouri. Nana sang in six different languages, and he couldn't get enough of it. After a road trip, you would pass him at 2 a.m. in the team van doing 40 kilometres per hour, and he'd be singing along to Anne or Nana. After I picked up the van, I would drive a route to pick up the six rookies attending high school and drop them off at school. The high school kids would hang out the windows and rock the van back and forth at every stop light. I was their "dad" taking them to school. After drop-off, I would switch cars with Killer once again and head to the gym to meet Dan. We would attempt to work out and then head to the steam room to relax. From the gym we would go out for lunch and then head to the rink for practice. After practice, we would have a light workout, talk for an hour, sit in the hot tub, then head to a local restaurant for dinner. The night would wrap up with us watching highlights while Dan enjoyed his chewing tobacco on the couch. Life was tough.

For that entire season we had optional pregame skates. A nice feature in Ottawa was that we had to wear only our helmets and gloves for pregame skates, and we could do whatever we wanted. There weren't ever any coaches in the building at that time. We would play a little 3-on-3 or just take some shots on net. Whenever my brother came down to visit, I would invite him out to skate with the team. I gave him one rule: don't injure anybody. By the end of the year, we were inviting bartenders from restaurants we went to and even members of the AAA baseball team, the Ottawa Lynx, to join us. We ended up trading favours with them. They'd let us join their batting practice and give us free tickets, and we did the same for them. I ended up befriending Ryan McGuire, who played for the Montreal Expos that season. After our season was over, he gave me and my brother field passes, tickets, and clubhouse access when they played the Blue Jays. It was another perk of playing junior hockey in Ottawa.

The food on the bus was a major point of contention with the players. Killer had a friend who owned the local KFC, and we were sponsored by Dad's Root Beer. It seems like a pretty simple explanation as to how 10 buckets of KFC chicken, five containers of fries, and two cartons of gravy became our pregame meal. Don't worry, we had two coolers of root beer and cream soda to wash it down. Most guys would peel the skin off the chicken and try to eat it plain just to get something in their belly, or they would eat at home before boarding the bus. After hearing our complaints for months, Killer said he would change things up. The next road trip, he walked on the bus with two big boxes of sandwiches his wife, Judy, had made at home. On fresh Wonder Bread, the options were tuna, egg salad, and ham. Now that will get you going. Killer brought some mayonnaise and mustard for those who needed it, and if you were still hungry after-wards, fans often baked us cookies for dessert. I felt like we were living in black and white.

We had a lot going on at the back of the bus. Nick Boynton and I opened a casino and had a $20 buy in. It provided a lot of laughs and the house won more often than it lost. We also created a game called dare/favour poker. We would play traditional poker, but instead of chips, we would come up with favours or dares that you had to perform.

For example, I take your bet of untying your skates after practice tomorrow and I raise you getting Gatorade for me for a week. It was hilarious and it got out of control. One dare had a guy tell Jeff, the owner, that he was too good for this league and he needed more money. For a week, I had to sing a song in another player's ear whenever Killer spoke during practice, which led Killer to asking me what the hell I was doing. Having your car warmed up for a week or your towel put in the dryer before a shower were perks of winning dare/favour poker.

We had a lot of fun and had the opportunity to celebrate things that other teams didn't. Coaches always gave players curfew on New Year's Eve, Super Bowl, and any other night that had the potential to be fun. Killer always let us do whatever we wanted, but if we screwed up, look out. That year we dressed up — inappropriately, looking back now — as pimps for Halloween, and we wore fur coats, top hats, and bell bottoms. We decided to stop in at Brian and Judy's to see his reaction to our outfits. Killer opened the door and said, "Judy, the boys are here. Get some food." We sat down on his couch and wondered if he even noticed our costumes. Judy came around the corner with snacks and a carton of milk on a tray. Brian looked at her sternly and said, "Judy, put away the milk, the boys don't want milk, they want a beer." He wasn't like any coach I had ever had before.

That season, a young public address announcer started out with the team. His name was James Cybulski, and he is now a well-known TV personality from both TSN and Sportsnet. James was a local kid who had recently graduated from Algonquin College. He was hilarious and he drove Killer crazy. Every game he would make an announcement that was way over the top, and he would give guys nicknames without anyone knowing. We were beating a team 6–1 and Brian Campbell scored the seventh goal. Cybulski announced, "The seventh Ottawa goal scored by Flyin' Brian Campbell, and what a goal it was!" Killer lost his mind on the bench, cursing under his breath, and he couldn't wait to find Cybulski after the game. He hated embarrassing other teams, as he was an old school coach in everything he did, and James had the persona of a wrestling announcer. One game, Cybulski called somebody the "ladies' man," and he would bring out various wrestling nicknames for the other players. He would do different voices on the PA and we loved it on the bench. Killer would yell at him throughout the year, but it didn't faze Cybulski one bit. He was a great guy, and I'm happy for his success.

It was during this time that I was rediscovering my love for hockey. I previously mentioned how people fall out of love with the game. People often say, "If I was that close to the NHL, I would've done anything to make it." Well, maybe. You probably have no idea of how much the mental and physical stress of the game and the homesickness of missing your family, friends, and girlfriend wears on you daily. The verbal abuse and the mental anguish are real. And you are young. You could be healthy scratched at any time. You could be put on the fourth line for practice to make a point. You could be forced into playing through injury without the proper medical care. Most people have no idea what it's like to ride the bus 16 hours a week and show up to school on four hours of sleep. Or know what it's like to be booed by fans or have the local newspaper call you terrible. If it were easy to make the NHL, everyone would do it. That is why very few people actually make the NHL and only a limited number of players come out of the game healthy. I hate it when people say, "I would've fought Tie Domi if it meant playing in the NHL." Again . . . maybe. But probably not. Tie rarely lost; he was terrifying. And guess what? If you won the fight, you would have to fight him again. Then others around the league would gun for you as well. Only when you come as close to the NHL as I did do you realize how much you have to sacrifice to have a career in hockey.

After a while, I didn't have that desire. The game had beat me down. But being in Ottawa helped me rediscover that passion. When I first got traded to Ottawa, I was introduced to a man named Laurie Boschman.

He was the first captain of the Ottawa Senators, and he played in the NHL for a very long time. Laurie was a tough player with over 2,000 career penalty minutes, but he also had over 500 points. Laurie was the chaplain for the Ottawa Senators, and through mutual connections in ministry, we were introduced and ended up meeting for coffee. We became good friends over my two years in Ottawa, and Laurie was in my wedding party many years later. I rediscovered my faith through my time with him, and I realized that I could no longer do everything on my own. I had a passion for the chapel program and guys on the team knew I was a Christian. Laurie and his wife, Nancy, would have me over for dinner all the time so I could escape my smoky house and relax. I finally found who I was again, and I remembered that I actually liked hockey. It was funny how Laurie and Killer, two men who were so different, would each have such a lasting impact on my life. Killer was funny with faith. One day, he walked through the dressing room and asked, "Do you want to have a chapel here?" I said that it would be great, and he said, "That's a good idea." Killer was open to considering his players' wants and desires because he was a players' coach. He was confident in his strengths as a coach, while still valuing the contributions of his players.

Now, if you thought our living arrangement couldn't have gotten any better, you're wrong. We acquired a vacation house to relieve our stress from doing nothing but playing hockey. Our owner, Jeff Hunt, lived in a huge house in the country, and when he went on vacation with his family, we would house sit for him as well. He had a hot tub and old school video games and pinball machines in the basement. We had the entire place to ourselves and the only rule was: *Do not touch the Porsche or the Land Rover in the garage.* Hey, we were mature young men and we had seen how *Ferris Bueller's Day Off* ended. That's why we only took the Land Rover into town and school. We had so much freedom at this point that we actually didn't go out that much, and we were in bed at a decent time. I was learning to live on my own and we had the responsibility of grocery shopping, paying bills, and doing all of our own laundry. It was the best year of my life.

There were so many funny things that happened over the course of my two seasons in Ottawa, that it is impossible to remember them all. I do remember a defenceman, Steve Lafleur, sticking a Labatt 50 label to the back of his helmet and wearing it for a couple of weeks, even on TV. He also tried to change his helmet number to No. 50. Killer never watched the warm-up, choosing to smoke a cigar with the opposing coach instead, so a couple of us would change jersey numbers in the pregame skate. The other team's assistant coach would write our lines down incorrectly, causing chaos at the start of the game. We got a little cocky, changed too many guys too often, and the league told us to stop. We played in London one night, and my best friend, Neal, and his girlfriend came to watch. In the second period, I dumped the puck hard into the zone to get a line change and the puck went over the glass. At that time, there wasn't protective netting, so shooting the puck over the glass was a common occurrence. After the game, I met Neal in the hallway and his girlfriend was limping and had a huge black mark on her pants. Out of the 3,000 fans at the game, I hit one of the two people I knew. Apparently, my buddy jumped out of the way, saving himself, and it hit her square in the butt. He saved the puck for me, but she didn't seem to find the humour in it.

As I mentioned before, Jeff Hunt was an amazing owner and he turned the franchise around within a short period of time. He was always looking for new ways to attract fans and rebuild our fanbase. Jeff implemented so many great promotions but I'll always remember his *Slap Shot* Night. He invited the Hanson Brothers to attend the game and I guess all it took was $5,000, three flights, a hotel room, and three cases of beer. The Hanson Brothers sat in our dressing room for the pregame speech and mimicked the entire shtick from the movie while Killer talked. I don't think he was impressed. They would blurt out, "We got a lot of losses," and "Like Eddie Shore," and we would be laughing but trying to stay serious at the same time. After all, we were about to play a game. The Hansons stood in the hallway before the game in full equipment, chirping the other team going onto the ice and giving them a couple light slashes on their shin pads as they went by. The brothers skated on ice for the pregame laps, taunting the other team in unison. Of course they stood on the blue line for "O Canada," just like the movie. I'll never forget Jeff Hanson looking at me and saying, "It's the F@&%ing anthem!" They were absolute clowns and the crowd loved it. They drank their beer and flew out the next day.

We were nearing the end of the season and we had just won the bid to host the 1999 Memorial Cup, so we were guaranteed a spot in the tournament. There was a mini celebration in the dressing room after finding out we had won the bid, but we knew we had business to take care of still. As a team, we knew we were good and we were currently the No.1 ranked team in the CHL. We were a tight knit group and not much would bother us. We thought we were prepared for any adversity. In the first round of the playoffs, we had very little difficulty advancing. It was easy and led us to believe that we would cruise into the Memorial Cup. That was short-lived as we had a hard-fought series against Belleville in the second round of the playoffs. The series was a battle, and eventually, Belleville came out on top. That loss created a huge time gap between the end of the playoffs and the Memorial Cup. I think we were missing that killer instinct in the Belleville series, knowing that we were in the Memorial Cup no matter what happened. Having that knowledge in the back of our minds prevented the team from fully reaching its potential in the playoffs. Belleville played with the desperation that we needed, as this was do or die for their season. This isn't an excuse, but I think it's the reason we were eliminated. We were beat by a team that wanted it more and would do anything to win.

In the weeks leading up to the Memorial Cup, I was approached by the local television station to host my own television show. The show consisted of me going out into the community and filming my day-to-day activities. On the second day of filming, I was doing a quick tour of the parliament buildings and I saw a crowd. I walked over to the group and realized it was for the prime minister of Canada, Jean Chrétien. Chrétien had just taken a bad fall playing basketball with the Canadian Armed Forces and had a huge cut on his head that was bandaged up. I snuck through his security detail with my camera, because that sort of thing happens in Canada. I reached out to shake the prime minister's hand, and he shook mine in return. I said, "Watch out for those stairs. They could be slippery and I don't want you falling again." He gave me a stunned look and thanked me. Thinking back on it, I was lucky I didn't receive a full takedown from the RCMP officers, but I ended up recording the whole interaction with the prime minister and it made the evening news.

With a week to go before the Memorial Cup, four of us went out downtown to hang out for a little bit. It was just an opportunity to get out of the house, and everything was pretty casual. We didn't want to stay out too late, so we called a cab around 11:30 p.m. As we were getting into our taxi, an altercation ensued between the driver and a teammate. Before I knew it, every taxi driver in the ByWard Market was charging at us and police cars were flying in with their lights flashing. I began having flashbacks from the Kingston incident. I tried to free up a couple of my teammates from the pile, but when the police arrived, they grabbed two of them and I snuck back into the crowd. I felt terrible as I watched everything unfold. While I was trying to figure out a way to fix the situation, a random civilian looked at me and said, "Probably not a good thing to happen before the Memorial Cup, eh?" Realizing there was nothing else I could do, I left before I got into any more trouble.

When we got to the rink the next day, we knew we were in serious trouble. A couple of the guys were in police custody the night before and we didn't know exactly what the team knew. If Killer found out, he was going to snap. We sat in the room and waited for him to walk into practice, but he was late. Killer was never late and it seemed like hours before he arrived. During the altercation the night before, someone's forehead got cut, which looked way worse because of the blood trickling down their face. When Killer finally walked into the dressing room he glared at us and screamed, "If you ever get into a street fight, you don't punch a guy in the forehead and let him bleed. You do three things: kick him in the balls, kick him in the balls, kick him in the balls. Get dressed!" He walked right into his office, and in his mind the situation was over. Publicly, he was asked about the incident and responded to the reporter with the following quote: "It has nothing to do with hockey. There's not an adult or kid alive that wouldn't want to take one day back in their life." He continued, "I don't think it will be a distraction at all. As far as I'm concerned, we're just here to play hockey. I hope the people that are here, are here to ask hockey questions. But if they're not, I'll give them the same answer as I just gave to you."

That was the best part of Killer: he knew the perfect way to deal with anything and there was nothing he hadn't seen before. I'm sure that he was scrambling to figure things out behind the scenes. He always had three pieces of advice to give when he was mad or was handling a situation. "Hey Davis, if you ever want to make that pass again, you can Fs%# off, F*&^ off, and F&*s off!" He could use it off the ice as well. "I heard you guys don't like KFC. Well, you can Fs%# off, F*&^ off, and F&*s off." It was classic Killer and you knew exactly when it was coming.

To be playing in the Memorial Cup in my last year of junior hockey, at home in Ottawa, was like a dream. I had endured so much in my hockey career so far, I felt like I was finally getting a deserved reward. I could never see the bigger picture at the time, but when I look back now, everything happens for a reason. From the Flamborough minor hockey chaos, to getting cut twice in junior, to the disaster in Sault Ste. Marie, I had dealt with more adversity than most people would deal with in their lifetime. I was resilient, and because of that, I now have very thick skin. I was going to do everything I could to finish my career on top, and this would include holding the Memorial Cup. I wasn't going downtown again until the tournament was over.

So what does a player do to prepare for the Memorial Cup? I'm not sure what everyone else was doing, but I was buying as many ticket packages as I could for my brother and best friend to sell on the street before each game. Neal was a good friend from Carlisle who followed me to every city I played in, and he was always there when I needed him. I bought 10 ticket packages for the tournament and figured if the scalping crew sold all of the tickets in a "grey area" price range, we would have enough money for a great vacation after the season. I knew that we would make the championship game, so we had the potential to make a lot of money. After all, I was still making only $45 a week playing junior hockey. I may not have been preparing like everyone else at that time, but it seemed like a great idea.

Our first game was against Acadie-Bathurst, the winners of the Quebec Major Junior Hockey League. It was an honour to start the first shift of the first game as I played on the top line with Mark Bell and Matt Zultek. Both of these guys were over six foot four and 200 pounds, and we formed a big, dominant line. Mark would go on to have a great NHL career, playing for Toronto, Chicago, San Jose, and a brief stint with Anaheim. He was one of my best friends in junior hockey, and he was a funny guy to hang out with. Mark and I would routinely grab poutine from Burger King, drive to my house, and play a lot of NHL '94 on my Sega Genesis. He is now an NHL scout, and I run into him every now and then around the rink in Guelph. Matt was also a great hockey player, and if it wasn't for a bad knee injury a year later, I know he would've had a great NHL career as well. Together, it was the best line I ever played on, and we dominated throughout the season.

Acadie-Bathurst had a good team, featuring Francois Beauchemin and Roberto Luongo. In the morning paper, I was asked about facing Roberto Luongo. I said, "It doesn't matter if it's Tretiak; if he can't see 'em, he can't stop 'em." Little did I know what that quote would foreshadow. My brother and Neal were a little late for the start of the first game, as they were out front negotiating ticket prices with the civilians. On the first shift, 49 seconds into the game, I took a bad penalty. Call it adrenaline, call it stupidity, either way it was the longest two-minute penalty kill of my life. It would set the tone for the tournament, and thank goodness we killed it off. We won the game 5–1, and I scored on Roberto Luongo in the third period on a tip in front with me providing the screen. I had to follow through on my prediction to the *Ottawa Sun*. I'm sure Roberto still remembers my goal to this day.

Our next game was against the Calgary Hitmen, owned by Brett "Hitman" Hart. Our team came out on top, 4–3, and we continued our great start to the tournament. We were 2-0, and we needed one more win to clinch a spot in the Memorial Cup final. Of course, we had to play our rivals, the Belleville Bulls, and we lost again in double overtime. I scored the first goal of the game, but we blew a four goal first period lead, and Belleville completed the comeback. If we had held on or even scored in overtime, we would've been one win away from being crowned champions of the CHL. Instead, we finished the round robin with two wins and one loss, booking us a spot in the semifinal against Belleville once again. If I said that we weren't nervous, I would be lying to you.

Much like the previous games against Belleville, we jumped to a 2–0 lead. They scored two goals shortly after, 20 seconds apart, and tied the game at 2. I'm sure that everyone on the bench was thinking, *Here we go again* . . . but Joe Talbot scored to make it 3–2, and it gave us a huge lift on the bench. Joe would later play with me at Western University, and he had a great hockey career. He would always show up in the crucial moments of big games. Before the end of the second period, I scored a big goal to make it 4–2 and provide a bigger cushion for the team. That was all the breathing room we needed, and we advanced to the Memorial Cup final on Sunday afternoon. Best of all, my ticket scalping crew would be able to cash in on the big win.

Killer invited the entire team to his restaurant after the game. Of course Killer had a restaurant in Ottawa — he had the key to the city, and everything else that he needed. As we sat down at the tables, six pitchers of beer arrived in front of us. Only in Ottawa would this happen. We looked at each other and said, absolutely no way were we drinking the night before the Memorial Cup final. We asked Killer if he could package them up for after tomorrow night's game. Killer laughed, and he knew we were focused and ready to go. This group didn't pass on free beer too often.

I slept great the night before the Memorial Cup final. I wasn't too nervous. It's funny, I just assumed we would win, and because of that, there wasn't a lot of stress. I stopped for my usual coffee and bagel, and I pulled the Taurus into the Civic Centre parking lot. That car had been through a lot with me so it felt like we were both making our last journey together. There wasn't a lot of life left in the old girl. I felt great in warm-up and everyone was just anxious to get going. Killer never wrote the names of the other team on the board in the dressing room before the game. In fact, we never usually saw him before the game until the pregame speech. When we came into the room after warm-up, someone had written the Calgary lines on the white board. The problem was, all of the names were spelled incorrectly and we could barely make out who some of the players were. We rolled our eyes and chuckled, and it loosened us up before the game. Calgary had an unbelievable player named Pavel Brendl, who ended up being the fourth overall pick in the 1999 NHL Draft. In our round robin game against Calgary, Killer asked our line to match up with him. He specifically asked me to keep an eye on him each shift and to shadow him if I had to. After a period of standing around watching him lazily float in the neutral zone, I looked at Killer and said, "I'm not doing this anymore. I want to play hockey, not stand around watching this guy." Killer replied, "That's fine with me." I loved that man, and we were going to do anything to win for him in his hometown.

The game was a back-and-forth affair with each team answering every goal. We were leading 6–5 with eight minutes to go, and Calgary tied it up at 6–6. Killer was unfazed by anything, so he pulled our goalie and put in our backup cold, with eight minutes to go in the third period. That was a gutsy call and the bench was a little surprised to say the least. The game headed to overtime and it was very tense in the dressing room. Matt Zultek was walking around telling everyone how nervous he was, and most of us were hoping we weren't going to be the one to make a stupid mistake and cost us the game. People stayed relatively quiet, focusing on what was ahead of us. Killer walked in silently, looked at the group, and said, "Somewhere in this room, there's a hero." He walked out and I could feel tears streaming down my cheeks. I don't know if it was the emotion of the moment or the adrenaline inside, but whatever it was, our team was ready to go. Killer gave the best pregame speeches of any coach I ever played for.

He spoke passionately and unscripted with his heart on his sleeve. That overtime speech was the perfect thing to say at that moment.

Dan Tessier's line started the overtime. Dan was a diminutive player who had a great vision of the ice, and he was the best faceoff man in the league. His line with my roommate Dan Tudin and Ben Gustafson were dominant all tournament as well. They were great all season but stepped it up during the Memorial Cup. One minute into overtime, Ben skated to the boards for a line change. The puck somehow ended up in the Calgary zone, down low behind the net. I have no idea how it got there. I gained possession of the puck and protected it with my body against the boards. I was always very good with using my size in board play and playing in front of the net. In the Memorial Cup, I dominated the boards and everything seemed to click for me. When the puck came behind the net, I noticed Matt Zultek streaking towards the net in the opposite direction that I was heading. I looked at the puck at my feet and fought off the defender behind me. I turned and sent a blind pass to Zultek in the slot, and he took the pass, deked the goalie, and banked it in off of his mask.

We won. We had just won the Memorial Cup, and I was on the ice for the winning goal. I stood frozen behind the net with my arms in the air. It was as if life stood still and I just wanted to watch it all unfold before my very eyes. We were the 1999 Memorial Cup champions and the crowd went nuts. My brother ran down to the glass and I tossed my stick to him so it wouldn't get taken in the celebration. A stranger grabbed my stick, but after a quick shakedown from my brother, he released it so Kyle could take it away.

In the post-game celebrations, I was presented with the Ed Chynoweth Trophy, which goes to the tournament's leading scorer. I had three goals and six assists. I laughed because the tournament MVP got a cheque for $1,000 and the leading scorer got a watch. Nick Boynton, our captain, won the MVP. He was much more deserving of the award than I was, but he had signed an NHL deal already and didn't really need the money — I needed the money. I sat on the ice against the boards long after the celebration was finished, just to soak everything in. It was a hard road to get there, but at that moment, it was worth it.

People say, "You are so lucky to have this moment," but they have no idea what I sacrificed to get there. During the champagne celebration, I remember locking myself in a bathroom stall in the dressing room and breaking down in uncontrollable tears. I thanked God for giving me this moment, and the previous 10 years flashed before my eyes. I had asked for help so many times, wondering why everything seemed to be going wrong for me. I was truly humbled by the moment, and I will never forget it.

Later on in the dressing room, I told the guys we should jump into the Rideau Canal with the trophy. Before the tournament, an Ottawa media guy told me we should throw the trophy into the canal if we won. He figured the backlash would last a couple of weeks, but the legend would last a lifetime. Unfortunately, the trophy never made it past the dressing room door. The handler said we couldn't take it out, so the idea was killed early on. That made our decision very easy, and we proceeded to run across traffic in our hockey underwear to cannonball into the Rideau. Later on, it was jokingly explained to me that we could possibly have contracted E. coli or hepatitis B from the dirty canal, but we couldn't have cared less. It couldn't have been any dirtier than the old Windsor Arena showers, or any old arena in the league for that matter.

When all of the crowds had left the building, and after I had said goodbye to my family, we headed upstairs to Killer's office with the Memorial Cup in tow. Five of us just sat in his office chairs, taking one cigar each from his box. We put our feet up and lit the cigars, doing our best Brian Kilrea imitations. We would move the names around the lineup board on his wall and say things in his voice, like, "Davis, he's terrible. Brutal skater and can't play physical. Put him on the fourth line." We sat upstairs in his office for an hour without a care in the world. Jeff Hunt eventually came into the office and said he needed the trophy from us. I bargained with him for five more minutes, to see if we could take the trophy out on the town. After some negotiating, we were told to have it back in one hour. I was in charge of the trophy, as I wasn't a big drinker, and I usually disappeared around 1 a.m. The Houdini act around midnight was my patented move. I was a responsible kid, and Jeff trusted me. My one request: I would need his new

Hummer to properly care for the trophy. We headed downtown in Jeff's Hummer, the Memorial Cup riding shotgun, to have the night of our lives.

The next morning, I woke up late and headed downstairs for breakfast. We had a team meeting later in the day, so I had to be up by noon. I sat down with a bowl of cereal and then I wondered . . . *Where, exactly, did I put the trophy?* I walked around the house and I couldn't find it anywhere. There was no sign of the Memorial Cup. I was screwed. *Please tell me I didn't throw it in the canal, please tell me I didn't throw it into the canal,* I thought. I called a couple of guys on the team to see if they happened to know where it went or if they had any idea where I could've left it. About 30 minutes later, I got a tip that someone saw Seamus Kotyk with at a Denny's around 3 a.m. Seamus was hilarious. He was the starting goalie and he wore a Burger King crown on the bench whenever he was backing up. He had a long career in pro hockey, and is one of the nicest people you will ever meet. When I arrived at the team meeting, Seamus came around the corner carrying the Memorial Cup, and I breathed a hugh sigh of relief. It wasn't in the canal after all.

The season wrapped up with a parade through downtown Ottawa on a double decker bus and Jeff Hunt taking all of the graduating players to New Orleans for the weekend. The trip was a bit of a sideshow, but it was a perfect ending to my time with the Ottawa 67's. So what did I learn during my time in Ottawa? I learned that it was possible to enjoy the game of hockey again. I learned that a coach could treat his players like human beings, value them, and take pride in their accomplishments. I had the opportunity to play for the greatest coach in junior hockey history, and he taught me who I was. The game wasn't always all about X's and O's. If you drafted well, and if you allowed your players to do the things that they did best, you could have a lot of success. I learned to take responsibility for my own life. Training hard, cooking meals, and learning when I needed sleep are essential skills that helped me mature into a better hockey player. I didn't have to call in curfew at 11 p.m. every night, and that freedom allowed me to have a life outside of hockey. So why does that even matter? Before I came to Ottawa I was depressed. I had anxiety and I was recovering from a second major concussion that affected my day-to-day life. I was like a beaten dog that looked for affirmation from anyone in the organization I was with. I rediscovered my faith and the direction I wanted to take my life. I knew that the next step in my life was out of my hands, but I felt prepared and equipped for whatever that step may be. In 2010, Brian Kilrea (with James Duthie) wrote a book called *They Call Me Killer*. He mentioned getting me from the Soo Greyhounds for a sixth-round pick, and that he always knew I could score. He praised my performance with the team and in the Memorial Cup final, calling it one of the best trades he ever made. That meant the world to me. I will never forget Killer.

My journey had taken so many twists and turns and I was barely 20 years old. It was enjoyable to go to the rink again, and I felt that minor hockey passion return from many years ago. The difference now was that I was finally comfortable in my own skin. It wasn't hockey that defined me, it was the fact that I finally felt like myself again and I knew what I wanted in the future. You may be thinking, *You won the Memorial Cup, you led the tournament in scoring, you assisted on the game-winning goal on one of the biggest stages in Canadian hockey, and you were so close to making it to the NHL. I would die to be in your shoes.* In fact, the NHL was the last thing on my mind. I didn't care what happened the following year. It was no longer my dream to make the NHL, and I wouldn't pursue that route unless I knew it was the right decision for me. Junior hockey had changed my outlook. Unlike many players who grind through the AHL and ECHL, I was no longer prepared to do whatever it took to make the NHL because, deep down, I knew I had lost that desire. Brian Kilrea rekindled my love of the game, and his coaching led me to rediscover my purpose and value, and that was enough. Maybe this was the end of the road for me, or maybe even bigger things were ahead, but I was finally excited to find out what was in store.

CHAPTER 8
CHASING A GIRL AND FINDING REALITY
(University of Western Ontario, 1999–2004)

After the Memorial Cup, I waited to see what offers were out there before I decided what to do for the next season. I had some interest from NHL teams but nothing great, and most of the offers I received were from the AHL and the ECHL. After the Memorial Cup, I had visited some schools out east and received some pretty good offers from Ontario universities. By the time August rolled around, I still had no idea what I was going to do and I couldn't care less. The AHL deals paid $65,000, but they turned into $18,000 if you were sent to the ECHL. I knew from my time with Washington that if I wasn't on an NHL contract, I would most likely end up in the ECHL making very little. My goal was to wait until mid-August to see if anyone offered me anything better. I actually had a sense of peace that I was going to end up in a good spot, and I wasn't anxious about it at all.

It was during this time that I started hanging out with a girl I knew at Muskoka Woods. We had known each other for years, but we were never really that interested in each other. It's funny, I met her parents earlier in the summer while she was dating someone else, and we had hit it off. I found out later that when her parents were leaving the camp, her dad had said, "Why doesn't Jessie just date someone like that Justin guy?" With two weeks to go in the summer, I asked her if she wanted to go out for dinner. Nothing serious, just the opportunity to see if we could be something more than friends. After the first date, we started talking a little more, and through our conversations, I found out that she was leaving for the University of Western Ontario (UWO) in London at the end of the summer. I remembered that the coach at Western had contacted me earlier in the summer, so I looked for his email address and his business card (yes, it was 1999). I eventually found the number for Clarke Singer, and I gave him a call, saying that I think I wanted to come to UWO. I asked Clarke if it was even possible to get into Western with three weeks remaining before school started and if my marks were good enough to get into the university. He said he would try his best, and one week later, I was on campus teaching hockey school and picking out my first-year courses. When Jess arrived for the first week of classes, I went over to her house every night to hang out. One night while she was in the bathroom getting ready to go out, I yelled out to her, "Hey! We should officially start dating. I'm at Western, too, now, so it only makes sense." Jess gave me some valid reasons why it wouldn't work out and why we may not be a good match, but I finished the conversation off by telling her, "That sounds great, Jess, but I won't be taking no for an answer."

I started university at the age of 21, fully prepared for school. My time in Ottawa with Ms. Kelly allowed me to work on my academics, and I regained my passion for learning. I was a mature student after seven years of high school, and I now had the necessary skills to succeed. At the last minute, my best friend from Carlisle and I found a cheap apartment on the outskirts of London. Neal and I negotiated a 12-month lease with the management, in which we only had to pay for the eight months we would actually be living there because we promised our cheques wouldn't bounce, unlike the rest of the tenants in the building. The landlord had one of the worst lazy eyes I had ever seen, and we could never figure out which one of us she was looking at during the negotiation process, so it didn't go smoothly. It was one of the funniest in-person negotiations I have ever been a part of, and we both left in hysterics on the way to our new home. Neal was the point man on my ticket scalping endeavour at the Memorial Cup, and we have had a lot of laughs over the years. It wasn't a fancy apartment or what the kids call a "clean" apartment, but it was a place for us to live. Later on in the semester, when my future father-in-law, Jim, came to pick me up for dinner, I had to tell him to meet me across the street from our complex, as the police had it cordoned off due to an ongoing hostage situation in the building. I was able to duck under the police tape to make our scheduled dinner while making quite the positive impression on Jim. Our safety was questioned at times, but the price of rent was fantastic. I enrolled at Kings College — an affiliated university college — at UWO to begin my university career, and I made my way to the main campus for kinesiology by the second semester.

Hockey started right away, and it was one of the few sports on campus that ran for the entire school year. We had a pretty good team in my first year, and Clarke had a great recruiting class. Darren Mortier from the Kitchener Rangers and Ryan McKie from the Sudbury Wolves were last-minute commits to Western as well. All three of us were late arrivals on campus, but it couldn't have worked out any better. The three of us formed a solid nucleus early on, bringing the hockey program much-needed exposure, and that allowed us to add some great players over our time at Western. We remain great friends to this day. I like to think that we had a big impact on what Western hockey is today. Much like the earlier part of my career, things seemed to happen for a reason, and I'm grateful for both of their friendships.

In our first year at Western we finished with a record of 19-4-3 and represented Ontario at the University Cup in Saskatoon. The team was 14-12 the year before we arrived, so our team turned things around. This would be the beginning of great things to come over the next five seasons at UWO. Hockey continued to be a lot of fun, and in retrospect, it was one of the best decisions I have ever made. I figured that I would have the same professional hockey opportunities after my graduation, and I would also have the advantage of having a degree in my pocket. Clarke was a brand new coach that season, and he allowed us to play our style of hockey. We were an unruly, talented team, who gave Clarke multiple ulcers with our on-ice and off-ice antics. Clarke did his best to rein things in each season, but our team was always a house of cards held together by a piece of Scotch tape. We recruited our friends, who recruited their friends, creating a sometimes-dysfunctional familial atmosphere where everyone was connected. It was a huge reason for our success, and I was lucky to be a part of it.

I'll be honest, it was a struggle for me to encapsulate this chapter of my story. Weeks went by as I tried to figure out how to succinctly wrap up the best five years of my life, while representing the impact it had on me. There wasn't a lot of negativity at UWO, as my coach followed through on all of his promises, and the hockey was actually enjoyable. All I kept coming back to in my reflections were the stories. Man, were there a lot of stories to tell. If there is one thing that hockey players have, it's the passion for storytelling and the ability to laugh at the same stories over and over again. It's one of the main reasons we play the game. I think of why I listen to the *Spittin' Chiclets* podcast and the reason for its success. People just want to hear stories about what it is like behind the scenes of the game of hockey. That is what civilians outside the professional game crave the most and what we former players hang on to dearly. I have a lot of respect for Ryan Whitney and Paul Bissonnette because they have the ability to reflect on what sucks in the game while reminisicing about all the things they miss about it. These are two guys who grinded out great careers in the NHL but saw the underbelly and nakedness of professional hockey. Listening to the podcast is like sitting in the dressing room with your teammates as you gripe about the practices, the coaches, and how your agent screwed you. Don't get me wrong, there is a lot of joy in the game and there are perks that come along with it, but what we all miss the most is the struggle and the time spent commiserating together. Oh, and we all miss the stories.

So that is what I keep coming back to when I think about this period of my life. Stories and lots of them. When you are in a great program like UWO, the leadership at the top sets the tone. I had great teammates, and we were all trying to win a championship together. Nobody had aspirations of playing in the NHL, as we had all collectively failed at achieving that goal long ago. Selfishness was removed because nobody was about to be traded or sent down another notch in the minors. We were adults now, and we had already seen every trick in the book, so Clarke couldn't manipulate us. He was forced to treat us as his family and actually have conversations with us. Even though we were now in university, we weren't 18-year-old freshmen living away from home for the first time. We were hockey players for the greatest university in Canada, trying to relearn how to enjoy the game and experience true freedom for the first time. There were no more 11 p.m. curfew calls or trade threats or drawn-out contract talks. My agent had forgotten about me long ago. So how do 21-year-olds react to this newfound freedom while balancing school and rediscovering the game they once loved? Well, do I have some stories for you.

Pizza Hut became an official sponsor of UWO Athletics in my first season at the school, and they offered a free personal pan pizza to the entire crowd whenever we scored six or more goals. Little did they know that we had five NHL draft picks, and our team was significantly better than the previous season. We scored six or more goals in four of our first six home games. By the end of the season, our crowd would be chanting, "Pizza, pizza," and we would all be busting our butts in a 5–1 game to score one more goal. We ran up the score on everybody in the Ontario University Athletics (OUA) that year, and we couldn't have cared less. In a 5–0 game with 30 seconds to go, we would put our top line on the ice, trying our best to score the sixth goal. When we would score, the on-ice celebration was like we had just won the Stanley Cup. Other teams thought we were arrogant, and they were right. It was the start of something great for Western hockey, and it became our identity.

We practised and played our games at the Thompson Road Arena on campus. It was handy to have our arena on campus and so close to class. The arena had portable seating that had to be pulled out for games because the ice was enclosed by a running track that the UWO track and field team used in the winter. Clarke would be explaining a drill on the whiteboard during practice and three attractive, very fit women would be running behind the glass every five seconds. This made everyone a drill killer (a teammate that didn't know the drill or who always did it incorrectly) at Western, and we spent the majority of our time trying to figure out what Clarke had said. Once in a while, a puck would be shot over the glass accidentally, and it would take down a runner on the backstretch of the track. It was hard not to laugh when a sprinter would collapse like a wounded deer after being struck square in the back with a puck. It led to a lot of arguments between the two teams, but we never did anything on purpose. Why would we try to injure the very people who made our practices more interesting?

Every year, Canadian University hockey teams would travel across the border to play against NCAA Division I schools. We were paid $5,000 to $10,000 for each trip, which significantly helped with the hockey budget for the upcoming season. If you ended up playing three games in three nights, you could make even more money on the trip. Unfortunately, because Western had such a good hockey program, only the top programs in the U.S. would put us on their schedule, since these games counted towards their overall record in the NCAA rankings. Therefore, we always played against Michigan, Michigan State, Notre Dame, and other top programs. With the trip being a bit of a money grab for us, we always managed to give our best effort in the first game of the road trip. By the end of the second game of the trip, however, the on-campus social life usually caught up with us. After all, it didn't count in our rankings, and it had no impact on our season. It was a great opportunity for my teammates to explore the differences between off-campus parties at an NCAA school versus the ones at Western. We liked to refer to this as a research gathering.

Our opening NCAA trip of my first season at Western took us to Cornell University. Cornell had a small arena on campus but it was jam-packed with the most obnoxious and organized fan base that I had ever seen. The entire pregame introduction was choreographed, and it involved newspapers and a lot of chanting and clapping. Much to our arrogant surprise, Cornell was a good team, very good actually. I think we touched the puck for a combined total of four minutes through the first two periods of the game, and we trailed 6–1 going into the second intermission. Early in the third period, the fans were dangling their car keys, taunting us with, "Start the bus, start the bus." Our egos were bruised as we knew we were much better than we were playing, so Eric Thomson touched off a line brawl leading to absolute anarchy. This sort of thing didn't happen in the NCAA, so the fans grew angry. I played with Eric for a short time in Ottawa, and we reunited at Western. Killer had nicknamed Eric "Rocky" because he was a hard-nosed player and he would fight anyone at any time. After the brawl, we returned to our dressing room and had a good laugh, even though we officially got pasted 7–1.

We decided to head out on the town and celebrate our drubbing, as our ability to immediately forget a loss became a big asset for our future success. I'll never forget that particular night starting out with one of our players accidentally dropping his case of beer at the top of a giant hill in downtown Ithaca. I can still see him chasing the cans one by one down the street, in the middle of traffic, dodging cars in the dark. At the end of the night, we all managed to regroup at a bar called The Dunbar. Our goalie, CJ Denomme, was an absolute nut, and he managed to get himself on top of the bar, while holding a bottle of Vodka to toast the entire crowd. The music stopped suddenly, and the bar became silent. CJ yelled out, "Here's a toast to Rick Sacchetti, he's our hero, Cornell scored seven but Rick scored zero!" Sacchetti was Cornell's captain at the time, and he was standing beside the bar in total shock. He had no idea who this clown was on top of the bar and why everyone was laughing at him. The music started back up and we were all dying of laughter in the back of the room. Before the bus dropped us off downtown that night, Clarke told us that the bus would be leaving from the top of the hill at 1 a.m. sharp. If you weren't on the bus, he was leaving without you. Morty managed to make alternative plans and he proceeded to tell Clarke at 12:59 a.m. that he was choosing to miss the bus, and he was taking six players with him. The next morning, two cars and one cab showed up at our hotel at 6:59 a.m., and the six missing players sprinted onto the bus, telling Clarke, "We're here, Clarky, we can head out now!"

As the season carried on, our team had the propensity to go out and act idiotic. This shouldn't be surprising for first year university students, but our average age that year was 23 years old, and we should've been the most mature team on campus. Like I mentioned before, this is the first time most of us had actually experienced true freedom in hockey. So what does acting idiotic and immature look like? Where do I even start? Guys would pour an entire shaker of salt on a random person's shoulder at the bar without them knowing and then walk away. We would empty an entire sugar container into someone's coat pocket, leaving them clueless until they tried to find their keys. Once a week, we would take a candle off of a dinner table and serenade an unknown couple at the bar with a rendition of "You've Lost that Lovin' Feelin'." The team would make a wall so the couple couldn't escape until we were finished. If you ever sat down with your girlfriend or you were talking to a random girl at a bar, you would have to scan the entire room for a moving candle, while searching for an emergency exit route in order to escape. It was a guarantee that the couple would be mortified. Shoe checks were constant at each meal, and the pranks spilled over into the team hotel. Guys on the team would go to the front desk and pretend to be another teammate who had lost their key and would ask the concierge for a new key to their room. When the occupants of that room had vacated the space, it was time to strike. We would take the fill valve out of the back of the toilet and point it forward, so when you flushed, it would spray out at you like a fire hose and flood the entire bathroom. Leaners were when you leaned a garbage can filled with water against the outside of the hotel room door. When the door opened from the inside, it would dump water into your room, soaking your feet and the carpet in the process. If there was a leaner on your door, you would have to call the players in the adjoining room to remove it for you. Another classic was taking all of the furniture from the room and stacking it in the bathroom. You don't think the furniture would fit into a hotel bathroom? Well, you're wrong, it fits perfectly. Sometimes, all of your pants would go missing or your room would be a sauna with the heat completely turned up. All of this chaos created non-stop shenanigans and an unbreakable team bond. It's what gave our team the formula for success.

University was going great, and I was finding my way around campus. I actually liked going to class and learning about subjects that I was interested in. Jess and I were getting along great and she fit in perfectly with my teammates and their girlfriends. Best of all, she didn't really enjoy hockey, so my time with her was an escape from the game. I thought I would dominate the league when I arrived at Western, as I came in as the leading scorer from the previous year's Memorial Cup and an NHL draft pick. I hadn't realized how good OUA hockey was and it was definitely a surprise. Eighty-five percent of the players in university hockey have played either junior or pro hockey, and their bodies are fully developed. There is a big difference between the strength of a 23-year-old and that of a 17-year-old. I enjoyed coming to practice every day. My enjoyment of hockey was at an all-time high.

Our team continued to play great hockey throughout the season, and we made it to the national championship in Saskatoon. It was the first time for Western in a really long time, and it was something we never expected going into the season. We began the season unranked and nobody at nationals knew anything about UWO hockey. When we took the ice for our first practice in Saskatoon, all of the teams were standing around the glass in anticipation of the new team from Ontario. They wanted to see us skate and to see what kind of talent we had on our roster. When the Zamboni was done flooding the ice, our goalie CJ Denomme came flying onto the rink. He was wearing a long black wig that was cascading out of his helmet, all the while faking that he couldn't skate. CJ was using choppy strides and falling down all over the ice on purpose, while the other teams looked on in disbelief. When he regained his balance, Clarke blew the whistle and called everyone to centre ice.

After every win that season, it was a tradition for us to play a game called "2 Puck." Basically, there were two pucks on the ice, we were all playing at the same time, and offsides and icings did not exist. Once both of the pucks were scored, you pulled the same two pucks out of the net, we had another faceoff, and the process started all over again. The first team to score five goals total was the winner. So, after CJ's sideshow Saskatoon introduction, our practice started with a spirited game of "2 Puck." After the first two pucks were dropped, guys began hammering each other, slashing sticks, cross-checking their own teammates, playing the body aggressively, and celebrating each goal like it was an overtime game-winner. Sticks were breaking and, like always, most of the losing team was boiling in anger. If I could've taken a picture of the faces of the players from the other teams watching our practice, it would've been priceless. The University of Western Ontario Mustangs had arrived at the Canadian Interuniversity Athletic Union National Championship and nobody knew what to think.

Our team competed hard during the round robin portion of the tournament, but we did not advance. In a decisive game, we lost 2–1 to the University of Saskatchewan, because of a goal that was called off because the ref said the puck did not cross the line. The next day, a photographer showed us a picture of the puck clearly crossing the line, but the moment had passed and it was much too late. To be honest with you, we didn't have the horses to win the national championship that year, but we were getting close. It was a great opportunity for us to see how we measured up against the best teams in the country, while enjoying a mini vacation in tropical Saskatoon. After we were eliminated, we learned that we did not fly out for another three days. Flights are always booked for everyone to depart after the championship game, so we were "stuck" in Saskatoon for the weekend. To have a team like ours stuck in a city, with nothing to do, was asking for a lot of trouble. I can vividly remember every time some-one would arrive back at the hotel after 2 a.m., Clarke would quickly open his room door and yell, "Go to bed!" We gave him the shakes in Saskatoon, and I think it took him weeks to recover from that one weekend.

Going to university was a great decision. At school, you end up in a place where everyone is on the same wavelength, in both hockey and life. Everyone on our team had played major junior hockey, and some had been drafted to the NHL. We all chose to forego professional hockey right after junior to get our education. Nobody was planning on leaving until they graduated, and we saw this as a four-year commitment to win a champi-onship. It was a great feeling to know that these would be your teammates for the next four years. We would all end up leaving school in much better circumstances than we arrived. If we went on to play pro hockey after graduation, we would have degrees in our pockets for when our hockey career was finally over. Too many of us had seen players over the age of 30 who were being released from their professional teams and had nothing to fall back on.

In junior hockey, you were drafted to a team without any say in the matter, and you didn't always have a lot in common with the other players. Players got traded or released, and the turnover rate was high. Likewise, there was an underlying selfishness in junior hockey, as you were there to fulfill your dream of playing in the NHL. In University, this was the team that you chose, and each season, you lost only three or four players to graduation or academic failure. Collectively, we were in this to win a national championship.

Each season, we had a couple of guys who would leave professional hockey and choose to play at Western. Some of them would succeed aca-demically, and others would spend $15,000 to forget the "class" component of attending university. They would fail out of school after one season and end up returning to pro hockey the very next year. Like the Trooper song says, they were "here for a good time, not a long time." Many chose Western for the same reason that I did, or to get away from the monotonous world of self sacrifice chasing the NHL dream. Early in my first year, I told Jess, "Don't get too attached to these people because when my four years are over, we won't stay in touch." Rarely does anyone stay in close contact with their junior hockey teammates after their careers have finished. Many of my teammates from Western are my best friends to this day. We were the best representation of a hockey family, and winning was the glue that kept us all together. All of the turmoil from my time in Kingston and the Soo led me to crave loyalty and family. I wanted to belong and feel like I was appreciated. My relationship with hockey was always a reflection of whether or not those needs were met.

We have a saying in hockey that our 50th best story is a civilian's funniest story of all time. So much time is spent together that you create a bond through mere stupidity. I feel sorry for the next generation of hockey players. Nowadays on the bus, players watch movies on their own phones and spend their time online instead of hanging out and talking to each other. We had to create our own fun, and we had to find a way to kill all of our free time. That's why we chanted on the bus and played euchre and schnarples in the pit. We had curling tourneys, team bowling events, and cheap Tuesday movie nights. That's why we found such enjoyment out of a loonie being glued to the floor. What we did to each other and what we did together was our social media. Ask any hockey player at any level what they remember the most, and they will tell you it's the time spent with their teammates.

The second season at Western brought even bigger expectations, as we added some great pieces to the team. My former roommate in the Soo,

Tim Zafiris, joined us from the London Knights. Tim is listed at five foot ten on Elite Hockey Prospects, but all of his former teammates would be quick to question that measurement. He was a great hockey player, who played angry, and he would fight anyone at any time. Tim was the type of player every team needed to be successful, as he held people accountable for their actions. The boys referred to him as "Bumble Bee Binky" because of his limited height and the one time he had an allergic reaction to being stung by a bee. Tim was the centrepiece of the next recruiting class, and he was a huge part of the championship run ahead. We also added Kelly Paddon that year, who played for the Belleville Bulls in 1999 when they beat us in Ottawa before the Memorial Cup. He was an offensive right shot defenceman who would anchor our power play for years to come. Kelly's nickname was "Doo doo doo doo do," as that is what we figured was going on in his head whenever he played. He would have the same body language after scoring a goal or creating a terrible turnover. The man had no pulse whatsoever, and his ability to not feel pressure in the biggest games of the year is what made him so great. When Kelly was working a summer job in his first year in London, he drove his delivery truck under the Talbot Street Bridge, eventually trapping the vehicle underneath the bridge and pulling the top off the truck like an open sardine can. He stepped out of the truck and slowly walked away. Eventually, Kelly returned to the scene and stood around with the gathering crowd, asking people, "What happened?"

We also added Andrew Power from Shreveport in the ECHL. He was a barrel of laughs and he had one expensive, memorable year at Western. We travelled to play Windsor early in the season for a regular season game. In Windsor, there was only one referee who could officiate university hockey. He was absolutely terrible, but we knew he would end up reffing every game we had there. And, yes, he would do his best to screw the visiting team. During this particular game, he had given us six straight penalties and we had played shorthanded for over two periods. Powey got a terrible penalty and it was the straw that broke the camel's back. On the way to the penalty box, he put his arm over his eyes like he was blind, turned his stick upside down like it was a cane, and proceeded to walk around the ice acting like a man without vision. He taunted the ref like this at centre ice for 30 seconds until he was handed a match penalty for travesty of the game. I have never seen anything like it, and the words "travesty of the game" represented the moment perfectly.

That year, I was lucky enough to play on a line with Darren Mortier and Rob Frost. At nationals the previous season, the hotel pranks in Saskatoon were so bad that Frosty would yell, "Arms in the air, state your business," before anyone came into his room. It became a running joke on the trip, and we formed a "coalition" to prevent our rooms from being damaged. We kept that nickname the next season and referred to ourselves strictly as "The Coalition." We became really good friends and spent a lot of time together. One night at the CPR Tavern in London, Darren was walking through the parking lot and ended up jumping on the hood of Frosty's Jeep to stop him from driving away. While Darren was standing on the hood, Frosty purposely hit the gas, sending Darren flying off the top of his Jeep and leaving him in a heap in the Ceeps parking lot. Ours was a different kind of friendship.

Frosty often did little things to bug his teammates, so when the team had finally reached their breaking point, players put "The Club," the steel bar that prevents auto theft by locking onto your steering wheel, on his Jeep, preventing him from driving for an entire week. Frosty learned his lesson the hard way and ended up apologizing for his antics.

Our team was extremely good that year. We finished with a record of 21-3 and advanced to the national championship in Kitchener. We were much stronger than the year before and we were better prepared to compete for the championship trophy. Everything seemed to be going according to plan until our game against St. Francis Xavier University, early in the nationals round robin, when we self-destructed. And by self-destruction, I mean self-sabotage at the Jean van de Velde level. St. FX was well coached and we had trouble getting control of the game. Their special teams and their systems were too much for us to overcome, and we lost 6–2. The reffing was horrendous, but it wasn't the only reason we lost. St. FX outplayed us and outcoached us, and we still weren't ready to be the best team in the country.

In retrospect, maybe it wasn't self-sabotage — maybe we just weren't good enough. The frustrating part was that we threw away our entire season in 60 minutes. After the game, our assistant coach lost his mind on the ref and followed him across the ice. When the ref told him that was enough, our coach gave him the throat-slitting gesture, like he was going to kill him. It obviously wasn't a good idea, but even worse, he was a teacher in London and had taken a sick day to be there with us. The next day, in the *London Free Press*, an article talked about the loss and mentioned our coach getting suspended with a gross misconduct for the violent gesture. He was a great coach and a mentor of mine, but much like the rest of the team, he was sometimes a little offside.

After the year ended, it was nice to finally relax and enjoy our limited time away from hockey. When the weather turned warm, we would sit around campus on the concrete beach or on the lawn at Morty's house on Oxford Street. The guys would pull some couches onto the front lawn and we would enjoy some drinks like regular students. Once in a while, we would grab a hairdryer from Morty's bathroom and pretend it was a radar gun, pulling cars over right in front of the house. It's amazing how many people think they have been caught speeding by a person wearing pajama pants and a tank top, pointing a hair dryer at them, with the cord hanging down. Another common practice was advertising "Free Puppies," in an attempt to get members of the opposite sex to join us. It turns out that women aren't overly attracted to or overly impressed by men who have deceived them. These antics kept us busy until exams were finished and everyone left for the summer.

Many hockey fans have been intrigued with the Carolina Hurricanes and their "Storm Surge" celebrations over the last couple of years. It's a novelty to hockey fans, but the concept is pretty simple: have fun, include your fan base, and enjoy the game of hockey. The videos of the team human bowling, fishing, and playing dodgeball are all things that we did at Western, both on and off the ice. Debates over whether or not fun should be allowed in the game is the reason why so many of us struggled through our careers. I'd never had more fun with a group of guys than during my second season at Western, even though our team was always hanging on by a thread. It's hard to believe that only four years earlier, I was close to quitting hockey. I was dealing with a major injury and serious depression and I hated hockey and the people in it, but now I loved going to the rink. I had completely changed my outlook on life and my relationship to hockey. My third year at the University of Western Ontario was going to be even better, and it would be a year that I would always remember.

Jess and I got engaged in the summer. I ended up moving in with four of my teammates in September because it was the last year before I would be married. We rented a house at 328 Cheapside Dr., and it was the focal point for all of our recruits for that upcoming season. We built a great team, and we were even better than the previous two seasons. The recruiting process would always start with steaks and drinks on our front porch. We would then take the player downtown to look at the scenery and finish the night off at Ceeps. The next morning, the player would call Clarke and tell him he was coming to Western for the next season. The place sold itself. We recruited eight freshmen for the upcoming season, and it was a talented group. Mike D'Alessandro and Matt Dzieduszycki came from Barrie, and they were both huge additions. Mike became our starting goalie over the course of the year, and Matt led the team in scoring and was an unbelievable talent. Joe Talbot, my old teammate from Ottawa, arrived as well. Joe played with Dewey and another addition from the London Knights, Ryan Held. They were our top line and carried us throughout the season. Tim Zafiris recruited his buddy Josh Bennett from the Kitchener Rangers, and Tom Brown arrived from playing pro. Josh was a tough, hard-nosed player, and Tom was a giant stay-at-home defenceman with the world's biggest can opener. Lastly, Chris Haskett came to us from pro hockey, and Shawn Thompson came from the Western League. Hack became one of my best friends, and he was a great all-around player. Shawn was a squirrely offensive defenceman with a tiny fuse. The roster was now full, and we had a lot of internal competition for playing time. *The Hockey News* ended up calling us the "most dominant team in hockey" at the end of the season, but it was a long road to get there. Talent was never a concern for us. The major concern was how Clarke would manage and control this group of misfits for an entire season.

The heartbeat of our team that season resided at a hockey house nicknamed "The House of Horrors." The guys who lived there made a lot of bad decisions, but they kept the team entertained with their stories. For example, halfway through the winter, the residents couldn't believe how expensive their bills had become. During their house meeting, they realized that they could save a lot of money if they just cut out the hydro bill. I wish I was the employee at London Hydro when they called to say they wanted their hydro cut in the middle of winter. When the hydro was cut a day later, they learned that hydro meant heat and electricity. When they called London Hydro back to say they needed their hydro turned back on, the employee said that they would send someone out in a week to reset it. The lady explained that they don't just turn hydro on and off whenever customers see fit. After freezing for a day, the guys decided that they needed heat badly. They found an old steel garbage can in the park and they loaded it with anything that would burn. They then started a fire in their family room. Yes, their new heating source was a bonfire inside their own house. A week later, the house remained standing and their heat was turned back on.

The residents of the house also played a game called "lashes." Basically, they would play *NHL '02* on the PlayStation and whenever someone lost, they would receive lashes from a belt. If they lost their game by three goals, the winner of the game could whip the loser across their bare back three times. They were a different level of wild. The house was an absolute asylum, and they were a reflection of our team. Let's just say, once a certain type of behaviour is normailized in junior hockey, it can take years to shake.

When we arrived at the rink, we practised hard. The internal competition drove guys to compete at a high pace as they worked to stay in the lineup. We knew how to separate the off-ice antics with our on-ice play. We pushed each other to be better, as we all worked towards the same goal. A huge addition to our roster that season, who didn't show up on the game sheet, was our new trainer Chris Maton. Mats was buddies with a couple of the players on the team, and Clarke recruited him to join our squad from St. Thomas, Ontario. It was one of Clarke's best moves during my time at Western, and Mats became a legend. We started calling him "Matman," and the team created a hanging flashlight in the ceiling that had a cardboard cutout of an "M." When he would enter the room, we would turn the lights out and Morty would play the Batman theme song on the stereo. If we put this amount of work into our schooling, we would have each earned our PhD. His jeans always seemed to hang in a straight line across his rear end, so players were often taken to Kangaroo Court for reportedly "stealing Mats's ass." He is now with the London Knights and has won numerous Memorial Cups. He was the 2019 Canadian World Juniors' trainer and represented his country with pride. We were so lucky to have him around, as Mats was a true professional who he treated us like gold even though we were long past our primes. I think deep down, Mats loved the chaos.

On the ice, our team was unstoppable. We ran the table on the year, going 24-0 with 135 goals scored and 40 goals against. We were essentially averaging a 5–1 win throughout the season, and that enticed *The Hockey News* to write an article about the team. We were extremely skilled, and we had the grit needed to win in the playoffs. There were players on our third line who would've been top point earners on professional hockey teams. Nobody ever complained, and we all had one singular focus: to win the national championship. The key ingredient to all of our success was our team bond, and the dumb things that made us laugh. We were doing things like the Carolina Hurricanes do now, which nobody else was doing at that time. Hurricanes fans stay around after an NHL game to watch their favourite players imitate a walkoff home-run, dunk a basketball, human bowl, fish with their sticks, or have a limbo competition. These celebrations may be intended for their fans but they also bring the players closer together. I had become an assistant captain, and I was in a great spot in life. If it was possible to pause life, I would have done so repeatedly that season.

What made us unique from any other team that I ever played on was our pregame process. When we arrived for a game, we would all go outside to play something competitive. We didn't just kick a soccer ball around or play catch with a football — we competed. Games of touch football or 6-on-6 soccer would end with guys trying to kill each other. This would lead to arguments about cheating or rule violations, and guys would actually yell at each other. After some blood was shed, everyone would return to the room, regain their composure, and grab a drink. Players would then tape their sticks or sit in the stands and watch the end of the men's league game. Five minutes before getting dressed, the whole team would gather for a huge game of hangman on the giant whiteboard in the dressing room. I was in charge of the puzzles, and two teams would compete against each other. Yes, that's correct, we played hangman before every game. The solutions would look something like this:

"Browny has a terrible haircut."

"Binky got stung by a bee."

"Who stole Mats's ass?"

"Why can't Frosty unlock his Jeep?"

"Keyzer runs funny."

All of these answers were funny things that represented game-day Kangaroo Court, and they would reveal secrets from the week before. When a player finally guessed the correct answer, the team would go nuts, and we would move on to getting dressed.

After suiting up, the coach of normal teams would come in five minutes before game time to give their pregame speech. They would share the opposing team's lines and give their tactical strategy to the team. If you ever watched 24/7: Road to the NHL Winter Classic on HBO, you would have some insight into normal pregame speeches. That was not us. Clarke had to come in 10 minutes before the game to give his speech because our assistant coach's starting lineup announcement took a minimum of five minutes alone. For example, he would say something like, "Starting on left D, he's a huge man, and somewhere out there, a zoo is missing his presence: Tom Brown." Morty would press play on the stereo and we would hear jungle sounds, with tigers roaring and monkeys howling away. One of the guys would walk around the room, imitating a giraffe. Someone would blow an imaginary tranquilizer dart into the giraffe's neck, and the giraffe would crumble to the ground. All the while, Tom would be sitting in his stall, laughing. Why would we do this? Well, Tom was six foot six, and we thought he was a huge man. That's it, plain and simple. We would find your weakness, and prey on it for the sake of humour and team bonding. If being tall was your strength, we could turn it into a weakness and the source of laughter.

Our sense of belonging on the team was connected to this humour. Self-deprecation and the ability to laugh at yourself was crucial to acceptance in the dressing room. An hour before we started the pregame introductions, players would secretly give our assistant coach bits of information about guys in the starting lineup. I laugh because our assistant coach was doing his masters in coaching at UWO, and his assistant coaching role was part of his education. Meanwhile, his pregame preparation was 45 minutes of information-gathering on the starting lineup. After introducing the first player, the coach would move on to the four remaining starters and finish with the starting goalie. By the time we hit the playoffs, we had to be dressed and ready 15 minutes before puck drop to get all of this in.

The team entered the playoffs on a roll, but we lost our first game at Lakehead University in Thunder Bay, Ontario, making the next two games must-wins at Western. It was our first loss of the season, and things were about to get much worse. We won Game 2 at Thompson Arena in overtime, with Morty scoring the game winner. As a team, we came up with the idea to play the Al Pacino pregame speech from *Any Given Sunday* before our games. We needed something different to change things up and we kept this tradition for the rest of our playoff run. After we had all left the arena to grab something to eat, our assistant trainer Lorne was doing the laundry in the dressing room and had a major heart attack. Lorne never regained consciousness and he passed away in our dressing room. We were crushed. We now knew losing wasn't an option in Game 3, but the game of hockey was suddenly put into perspective. It was an emotional pregame in the dressing room before Game 3 until we pressed play on the Al Pacino speech once again. In the near silence, guys were fighting back tears and the message became clear: win this one for Lorne. There was an emotional ceremony for Lorne on the blue line before the game started, and we went on to win the game easily. The entire team attended Lorne's funeral days later, and we had a patch sewn onto our jerseys for the rest of the playoff run.

We eventually advanced to the national championship in Kitchener a few weeks later, and it was an exhausting period. In the last minute of the Queen's Cup final (the Ontario University Championship) I took a soft chip behind the net and iced the puck on the penalty kill. After I released the shot, I got hammered into the endboards and I immediately knew something was seriously wrong. I had separated my shoulder, and I was crushed, as this was my best opportunity to win the national championship at Western, and I was injured and unable to play. I decided that I would take a week off and assess the situation before we travelled to Kitchener. If I could somehow play with my shoulder frozen, I could endure the pain that came with it. The doctors told me that I could risk further damage to the shoulder, but the damage would be minimal, as it was already a first-degree separation. The only real problem was pain management, and I hated needles.

During the first practice at nationals, I realized that it was too painful to shoot the puck. I skated around by myself during drills, just to keep up with my conditioning and to feel like a part of the team. I dressed for the first game and took warm-up without freezing. I ended up stickhandling a little bit, but I stayed out of the line rushes. When the warm-up concluded, I went into the medical room where the surgeons from the Fowler Kennedy Clinic in London were waiting. One of the surgeons in residency was Frosty's brother, Sean. The doctors injected the injured shoulder with an anesthetic, so I couldn't feel a thing. My entire upper body was completely numb, and it took a while to get used to the dead-arm feeling. I continued this process throughout the tournament, and I began to dread the pregame needles more than the excruciating postgame pain. We advanced to the semifinals of the tournament and faced a really good University of Alberta team. Alberta was the number one team in the country at the time, and they had won two of the previous three national championships. In the semifinal game, Mike D'Alessandro faced 15 Alberta shots in a lopsided first period, and he stood on his head. We were confident that we had the best goaltender in the game, and that was a huge advantage for us going forward. Joe Talbot tied the game up at 1 with a shorthanded goal just before the period ended. During the first intermission, we locked the dressing room door and shut out all of the team staff. We had a heart-to-heart as a team and essentially forced ourselves to look at the opportunity we were throwing away with our first period effort. All of the time spent together as a close-knit family enabled us to deal with this adversity. After the closed-door meeting, we came out flying and never looked back. Our team bonding and shenanigans throughout the year were vital at this moment, and the only people who were able to connect us were the guys in that room. We won the game 4–2 and frustrated Alberta in the last two periods with our suffocating team play. We had one more game to win to reach our ultimate goal.

We faced off against Université du Québec à Trois-Rivieres in the national championship game for the University Cup. The game was on a Sunday afternoon at the Kitchener Auditorium. If we had one rival at Western, it was UQTR, as we always seemed to face off against them in the Queen's Cup championship. We had lost by a single goal in the three previous matchups, and much like Belleville in the Memorial Cup, they had our number. After the first period, we found ourselves with a 3–1 lead.

UQTR tied things up in the middle frame, and the third period finished scoreless. We were headed to overtime for the national championship, and it would be the second time I would need extra time to settle the outcome in a title game.

After regulation, I went in for more anesthetic, as I was in a ton of pain. The medication would usually last for three hours, or the length of a hockey game, but with the commercials from the broadcast, this game dragged on a bit longer. The medical staff injected me again and gave me medication to control the pain. When I returned to the room, the team was focused. During the first overtime, UQTR had a breakaway to win the game that Dally made a great stop on. The period ended scoreless, and we were headed to a second overtime. During a commercial break in the second overtime, I was sitting on the bench and I heard the in-house entertainment crew interviewing a fan for a contest. I recognized the voice on the PA right away, and, of course, it was Jess. She had had her bachelorette party the night before in Kitchener, and she was at the game. Jess was wearing a veil and holding a sign that said, "#10 in the program, #1 in my heart, I DO." Her friends made her bring it in, and her interview was extremely embarrassing due to the seriousness of this being the second overtime of a championship game. The guys on the bench were looking at me in horror, and I just shrugged it off with a laugh. With three minutes to go in the fifth period, Clarke tapped Chris Haskett on the pants and said, "You're up." Hack responded, "I'm done, Clarkie. I have nothing left, send someone else." His legs had seized and cramped up, and many of us were starting to feel the effects of the short tournament format. Hack became our biggest cheerleader on the bench.

Before the third overtime started, I went in for my third injection of the game. This was not what I had planned, but I could hardly lift my arm due to the pain. I was dead weight for my line, and I felt bad for "The Coalition." I was basically chipping it in and chipping it out for the whole second overtime, like my Swervin Ervin days in Junior C. I had become the all-time high guy in the zone, and I just held the fort for 30 seconds so the other right wingers could rest. My shoulder was numb once again, and we headed out for the sixth period of the game. We had a good crowd of around two thousand people for the championship game, but the Kitchener Rangers were scheduled to play at 7:30 p.m., long after our 2 p.m. start. Now, five hours later, we had a full house for the sixth overtime, as fans had arrived for the OHL game. Of course, everyone was cheering for the local team from Ontario, and it was a boost for our team. On a faceoff early into the sixth frame, Kelly Paddon took a point shot after a won draw by Jeff Hare, and he fired it on net. Stacey Britstone grabbed the rebound and buried it in the back of the net. We were the 2002 national champions. The bench emptied, and over 200 fans from Western poured onto the ice like a college football game celebration. It was a moment like none other, and I wouldn't have expected anything less from this squad. We boarded the bus after the game and headed back to the University of Western Ontario as national champions. Other than the trophy sitting on the Euchre table, the group was relatively subdued and exhausted. We went out to the Ceeps when we got back, but most of the guys headed home earlier than ever before. We would save our celebrations for the weeks to come. By 1 a.m., all of the anesthetic had worn off, and my shoulder was a mess. It would take a long time to heal, and I still feel the repercussions to this day. The "minor complications" the doctors had explained to me before the tournament keep me up most nights, but that win makes everything seem worth it.

Over the next week, the University Cup made it everywhere in London. We turned the trophy into a dance floor, allowing people to dance inside the Cup until all hours of the night. This was a great idea until the entire top of the trophy came off on one particular evening. Joe Talbot took the pieces to his grandfather's apartment at 1 a.m. to have him weld the trophy back together before we got into serious trouble. During that season, there was a parking attendant named Russ who controlled the Thompson Arena parking lot. Russ was the gatekeeper, and if he didn't like you, you had to find somewhere else to park. Campus parking was difficult and very expensive at Western, so it was important to keep Russ happy. When you pulled up to the gate, he would pull out his *Hockey News* and spend 10 minutes giving you advice. Even if you didn't want to listen, Russ wasn't going to lift the arm of the gate until Russ was ready. There would be 10 cars backed up trying to get into the parking lot, and he would be showing you the Bob Mackenzie article on who was going to get traded next week. He loved the team and we gave him some good laughs. As Joe was carrying both pieces of the destroyed University Cup through the hallway, Russ the parking attendant peeked his head out of his own apartment and shook his head in disgust. Apparently, Russ lived in the same building, and as always, he never missed a thing. A couple of weeks later there was a reception in our honour at the university president's house, and we were also honoured at King's College. Nobody seemed to notice the newly welded lines barely holding the trophy together. In class one day, one of my geography professors made me stand up as the entire class clapped for me. He congratulated me on the accomplishment, and I was surprised that he even knew the school had a hockey team. We were minor celebrities on campus for the rest of the school year, and it was a great feeling.

Every couple of years, I always make an effort to take some time to figure out how I arrived at this stage in my life. I find it fascinating to analyze what I'm currently doing and look back on how I got there. In 1999, could I picture myself getting married in three years, being close to graduating from university, and winning another championship? Of course not. I thought I would be playing professionally somewhere, clinging to a dream that I would never achieve. 2002 was one of the best years of my life on a personal and athletic level. I was growing up quickly, learning valuable lessons, and becoming comfortable with who I wanted to be in life. If you can't reflect on the positives and negatives of your past and the process it took to get there, you can't grow as a person. I could finally look in the mirror and see someone I liked looking right back at me. There were a lot of obstacles on the way, but adversity seemed to define me.

The following two years were a lot of fun and we had some great teams once again. We never made it back to the national championships but we had a lot of success. We continued to travel to the U.S., and in 2003, we had the opportunity to play at Notre Dame against the Fighting Irish. Chris Haskett was from Lucan, Ontario, and the town's sports teams were known as the Irish. He drove a '93 Buick LeSabre with the plushest seats known to man. The 10-minute drive from the rink to my place each day as we solved the world's problems is one of my best memories at Western. Chris had a leprechaun tattoo on his arm, and the trip to Notre Dame was a big deal to him. We arrived on campus in South Bend, and we checked in to our hotel. We didn't have initiations at Western, and our rookie parties consisted of casual drinks and first-year players doing a skit that made fun of the veterans. Everyone had a job to do on each road trip, so I chose to be the guy who does a player headcount on the bus before a trip. That way, I never had to carry any equipment or do any manual labour before the game. My only job was to make sure everyone on the team was present before we departed to wherever we were headed. Our team had a tour booked at Notre Dame Stadium for this particular trip, and a university representative was going to take us onto the field. Hack and I left our room together and we walked towards the team bus. Clarke asked me if everyone was on the bus, so I did my usual fake head count, and then I said we were good to go.

After the tour, we walked onto the 50-yard line. I told Hack to kick a fake 50-yard field goal, as this was his legendary move at Western. Whenever we went out, after the bar would clear out late at night, Hack would put down an imaginary tee. He would then place an imaginary ball on the tee and count his steps backwards. After staring down the imaginary goalposts, he would trot forward and kick the imaginary ball as far as he could, and the bar would erupt. I would signal that the field goal was good. When Hack didn't answer me on the 50-yard line, I knew something was wrong. Apparently, he never made it onto the bus, and I could only imagine his anger as he stewed in our hotel room. It was an anxious and awkward bus ride back to the hotel, and when I arrived to our room, he said to me plainly, "You are an idiot." I learned my lesson until I forgot him again at the pregame meal two days later. Hack was standing in the parking lot of the Italian restaurant all alone, shaking his head in disbelief, as the bus was pulling onto the ramp of the freeway. I decided right then and there it was time to start counting correctly.

School was always a challenge for the team, but some of us took it seriously. We were in good programs and needed to keep our grades up to stay. Others just wanted to graduate with a degree and find a good job after graduation. Morty was one of the latter, but one night, he was looking for something to do and decided to attend class. He showed up to three or four classes a semester, but he made sure to attend all of his exams. I would be studying my butt off in the King's College library and I would hear loose change clanging away like I was at a laundromat. Then I would hear the photocopier humming for two straight hours. I didn't have to get up to know it was Frosty and Morty photocopying random girls' class notes from the five courses they never attended that semester. So when Morty showed up to class that night and sat beside Jess and a player on our team, it was surprising. When the professor walked in, he opened his notes and started the lecture. About a minute into class, he looked at Morty and said, "Excuse me, are you in the wrong class?" Morty said, "No I'm in this class." The professor told him that he didn't remember him, and Morty stood up and walked out. That was one of the last times he attended a class at Western.

Midway through my last year, we were heading into the U.S. for another NCAA weekend. The bus pulled up to the border and a customs agent boarded the bus. This was at a time when an agent would stand at the front of the bus and ask the entire team if everyone was Canadian. He would then ask us to hold our passports up in the air for him to see. The agent would nod his head and leave the bus right away without checking anyone's identification. On this U.S. trip, I happened to forget my passport, but I wasn't too worried as nobody ever checked. Of course, this was the trip when the agent decided to go player by player and look at each individual passport. When he got to me, I showed him my driver's licence and he proceeded to take me off of the bus. Clarke came in with me in case I couldn't cross the border. I was taken into a room with a two-way mirror, and I was seated beside Clarke. An agent came into the room and asked for my full name. He then asked, "Are you the Justin Davis wanted for double homicide in Saskatoon?" I quickly answered, "No." He followed that question with, "Are you the Justin Davis who broke his parole for the armed robbery of a TD Bank in Thunder Bay?" Again, I answered, "No." His last question was, "Are you wanted for sexual assault in Brandon, Manitoba?" Quickly, I answered, "No." The agent said he would return, and he left us together in the room. I looked at Clarke and whispered, "I had this incident five years ago in Kingston involving an assault with a deadly weapon. It wasn't good but my lawyer said it's expunged and it's long gone. Just play stupid if they say something about it." His face went as white as a ghost, and I thought he might faint. The agent returned five minutes later and said, "Mr. Davis, you are good to go." We walked out of customs and onto the bus. I received a round of applause and multiple chants of "He shot a baby," that were referring to my paintball allegations from years before, but the Mustangs were back on the road.

In my last season as a Mustang, I had the privilege of making the OUA All-Star team. Our team had the opportunity to play two games against the Canadian World Junior team in Kitchener over the Christmas holidays, before they left for their tournament in Helsinki. Team Canada had Sidney Crosby, Brent Burns, Mike Richards, Ryan Getzlaf, Brent Seabrook, Dion Phaneuf, and Marc-Andre Fleury in net. Although I was quite a bit older than most of these players, I made it a point to finish my checks on everyone and to try to score on Fleury. I realized that this was the only time I would get to give Sid a little slash on the top of his laces on a faceoff, as we seemed to be headed in different directions with our careers. We lost both of our games in Kitchener, but it was a lot of fun to see the early potential of a future Hall of Famer.

I finished my career at Western in 2004. I was the captain of the team, and I was attending teachers college and wrapping up my time at the university. Jess had been accepted to teachers college as well, and we were living in an apartment on Talbot Street. It was the year of the double cohort in Ontario, which meant first-year students were entering university at 18 years old now, and it was time for the married 25-year-old to move on with his life. I was fortunate enough to finish my career at Western as the all-time leading scorer, scoring 42 goals and notching 81 assists. The total of 123 points in 83 games is something I'm extremely proud of, but it is the national championship that means everything. I cherish the opportunities that I had at Western, and I am grateful to Clarke Singer for everything he did for me. He is a great man whom I hold in high regard, and I am thankful for the life-changing experience he provided for me at UWO. I met my best friends, I graduated with a teaching degree, I won a Purple Blanket (given to athletes who achieve superior distinction at the national level as representatives of Western), I won a national championship, and most importantly, I married Jess. It was the greatest five years of my life.

CHAPTER 9
DEUTSCHLAND
(SCM Neuwied, 2004–06)

After graduation, Jessie and I continued to live in London. We were supply teaching to make some extra money, and we were waiting to see what was in store for the upcoming season. We now had our teaching degrees, and that gave me the opportunity to spend the next couple of years exploring any professional hockey opportunities that were available. I contacted my agent and asked him if he could find out what was out there, and I would then evaluate what I wanted to do. My agent came back with the same offers that I had before I went to Western, and it was an easy decision. Did I want to play 72 games in the AHL with New Orleans for $18,000 a season and extensive bus travel? Did I want to spend three more years pursuing an NHL dream while dragging my wife around the continent? The simple answer was no. I knew I no longer had what it takes to make the NHL, and time and potential was no longer on my side. I came to the conclusion that hockey had used me for so long, it was my turn to use the game of hockey to benefit me. I was going to play in Europe and see the world. Since we got married so young, Jess and I didn't have a lot of money, so we could use this experience as our extended honeymoon. My main focus became signing with a European team that:

1) had a Canadian coach
2) was located in central Europe, for easy travel opportunities
3) offered a contract with car, apartment, and minimum 3,000 euros a month
4) provided flights, unlimited sticks, equipment, and a work visa for Jessie
5) scheduled one road game and one home game a week

I hired an agent named Drago who Morty had used in his previous year in Germany. He was Slovenian and had connections all over Europe. The sleazy part of European sports is that the agent, the coach, and even the general manager all get a cut of your deal. I didn't know much about Drago, but I did know that he had previously helped some of my friends find some great situations in Germany. Drago only called me by the name "Champ" whenever we spoke on the phone. I just assumed he forgot my name or he had no clue who I was. I met Drago only once in my life, and that is when I owed him 2,000 euros in contract fees. He arranged to meet me in Stuttgart, Germany, to collect his money. When the bus pulled up to the Stuttgart Arena, there was a little man waiting on the sidewalk. He was pacing beside the bus as the bus driver finished parking, and when it came to a full stop, he stood directly in front of the bus exit. As every player walked by he would greet them with, "Hey, Champ," until I finally stepped off and greeted him with a handshake. We talked briefly, I handed him an envelope with the cash, and he drove away. It was one of the shadiest interactions I have ever had in my life, and I wondered for a couple of weeks if I just gave 2,000 euros cash to a random stranger in Germany. After every big weekend that I had that season, the phone would ring on Monday with, "Champ, it's Drago, let's get you a bigger deal next season!"

So it was in my initial talks with Drago that he found me the perfect situation in Germany. The team was called SCM Neuwied and it was located 10 minutes from Koblenz, where the Rhine River meets the Moselle River. Neuwied was a small industrial town, but it was the perfect location for Jess and me to live. We were given a small apartment in Ehlscheid, five minutes away from the arena, high up in the hills. I received 3,000 euros a month, and something tells me Drago made a little bit of extra cash on the side of our deal, but we were happy. Each team in the Oberliga is allowed five import players. We had two Finnish players, a Slovakian player, and another Canadian. It was a great mix of guys, and much like Ottawa and Western, the team was a perfect fit. We flew to Germany in August for training camp, and little did I know what was ahead of us for the next couple of years.

When we moved into our apartment in Ehlscheid, we assumed we would find somebody who spoke English. We couldn't have been more wrong. The people in the building were quite old and they had no time for the young Canadians. Notes were left all around the building with, "Kanadisch, nein . . ." Basically, Canadians, whatever you are doing, it is wrong. Garbage disposal, wrong. Laundry, wrong. Parking, wrong. I had to recruit a teammate to act as a delegate for Jess and me. Our neighbour downstairs was Tyson Mulock, 21-year-old from North Delta, B.C. He was an amazing hockey player and we played on the same line for the whole season. We adopted Tyson for the year, and we carpooled together, watched *The O.C.* together, ate dinner together, and travelled around Europe as a family. I was a little homesick at the beginning of my time in Neuwied, so I couldn't have imagined being him, a young Canadian player living alone in a foreign country. The team gave us our team car, a manual Mitsubishi Lancer. Jess and I weren't able to drive stick shift at that time, but we faked it out of the dealership. After a couple of hard bunny hops and a few stalls, we were back on the road to Elscheid.

Our arena in Neuwied was from the 1970s. It was small, and it had mesh netting behind the nets instead of standard glass. During warm-up, somebody would blow cigarette smoke in your face if you didn't turn your head away quickly enough. During a home game early in the season, I dumped the puck hard and high into the corner. The puck hit the mesh and it rocketed out like a slingshot. My brother was at the game, and he said the guy standing beside him in the same corner was criticizing my play the whole period. When my dump in hit the netting, the mesh moved backwards and the puck hit the fan in the forehead, creating a huge gash on his face. My brother said it couldn't have been more perfect.

The fans were fantastic, and it was a totally different atmosphere than in Canada. The game would begin with player introductions in the dark, while every fan held a sparkler or flare and lit bonfires in the stands. Constant drumming could be heard from the pregame intros right up until the end of the game. The PA announcer would introduce each player individually, "Nummer zwolf, Justin . . ." and the crowd would scream, "DAVIS!" If we won, all of the players would come back onto the ice in our half equipment. You had to skate around the perimeter of the ice surface, high-fiving every fan in the crowd, while receiving a complimentary glass of beer from the fans every five minutes. One night after a big win against a rival team, the fans were chanting for 10 minutes after the game. I asked the German player next to me in the dressing room what they were chanting. He looked at me and said, "They want the caterpillar." I asked him to explain what the caterpillar was, and he said, "You'll see." The entire team proceeded to go back onto the ice and we got down on our hands and knees. Each player grabbed the ankles of the player in front of him, and we formed a giant caterpiler, crawling around the ice. The crowd went absolutely nuts, and I was in utter disbelief. I was a long way from home.

The hockey was a huge transition for me, as the game was very different than what I was used to. Practices were designed much differently than in Canada, and our style of play involved a different way of thinking. For example, in junior hockey we were always taught to gain the red line, dump the puck deep, and then go get it. The first time I dumped the puck in, the Slovakian player beside me on the bench said, "We have puck, you give them puck. Keep puck." From then on, I gained the zone with possession of the puck. Likewise, I think I led the league in offsides and pulled groins for the first two weeks of the season. I would always go hard at the blue line to retrieve the expected dump in from a teammate, but the puck carrier would suddenly turn back towards our own end at the last second if they didn't like what they saw at the blue line, and I would have to slam on the brakes. Other times, the puck carrier would make multiple moves at the blue line, leading to another stoppage in play caused by the new Canadian. In Canada, we were always taught to dump the puck into the zone, in order to change. When the team wanted to make a line change in Germany, the defenceman would just set up behind the net and the other four players would change. The new defenceman skating onto the ice would take possession of the puck, and the tired defenceman would head off for a change. Now, our team still had the puck and we were fresh. After a while, these concepts made complete sense, and I realized many aspects of Canadian hockey were strategically wrong.

Our team was in the middle of the pack for most of my first season. We had some really good import players, but we weren't paying as much money for these players as the top teams in the league. European hockey is funny this way, as some teams want to win but they don't want to win the league championship. The main reason for this is the relegation system in European sports leagues. Each season, the bottom two or three teams in every German hockey league move down one division. Likewise, the top two or three teams in each league move up one division. For a North American example, it would be like the Detroit Red Wings moving down to the AHL next season and the Toronto Marlies moving up to the NHL. This creates a system where the middle of the road teams try their best to avoid both relegation and promotion. If their team were to get promoted to a better league, the budget jumps and the price of the infrastructure climbs, and not every team can afford the promotion. The goal becomes to beat your rival teams and to avoid relegation. The budget for each team is based on community sponsorship. Teams don't have an affluent owner who can cut the cheque for the entire season, so the money comes from local business sponsorship. For example, the sponsor on the front of the jersey is worth

$800,000, the sponsor on the pants is worth $500,000, the shoulder sponsor is worth $200,000, and the helmet sponsor is worth $100,000. The remaining money is made from the ice and board sponsorship for the entire year. Out of this overall budget, teams spend a lot on import players while trying to get cheap German players. This creates a system where the best teams have the best imports and the highest paid German players. In Neuwied, we had really good import players, a couple of good Germans, and the rest of the guys were on the roster to provide a breather for the top players. This was a lot like my Junior A days in Flamborough. I never came off the ice that season in Germany, and the team relied heavily on the other import players as well. If you didn't perform as an import player, the team would find a new player to replace you right away. There was a ton of pressure to play your best.

Ladislav Strompf was one of my favourite import players from that season in Neuwied. He was a 36-year-old Slovakian defenceman who had a long, distinguished career in Germany. He was a unique individual to say the least. Latso would always have chewing tobacco in his mouth when he played, and by the end of a practice, the ice surface would be covered in brown spit. Sometimes the puck would hit you in practice and you would have to wipe the Latso chew off your pants. If we were ever out late after a game, Latso would invite the entire team over to his house for a late night snack. We would walk into his house quietly, so we didn't wake his kids, and Latso would go upstairs and wake up his wife. At 3 a.m., his wife would come down the stairs in her pajamas because "the boys are hungry." After making a meal for everyone, she would return to bed. It was always an awkward situation for me, but it was a great meal. I could only imagine waking Jess up at 3 a.m., asking her to feed my friends. I'm sure her answer would be along the lines of Brian Kilrea's favourite saying: "I have three answers for you . . ." One Valentine's Day, I asked Latso what he was getting his wife, and he responded with, "Valentine's Day is for people in love, not people who are married." The man was a Slovakian Socrates. Jaroslav Majer was the other Slovakian player on the team, but he counted as a national player because he had a German passport. Jaro and

I communicated in broken German, and we seemed to understand each other quite well. I often wonder what happened to these two individuals and what they are doing today. Hockey has a way of bringing fascinating teammates into your life.

Road trips in Germany were very different from anything I ever experienced in Canada. In our league, we always played one road game a week, either on a Saturday or a Sunday evening. Our home games were consistently on Friday nights. During that first season in Neuwied, my brother flew in to visit. We picked him up at the train station in Koblenz, and he hopped on our bus for our road game. I made Kyle a bed in the aisle of the bus, and he slept for three hours. Family member didn't usually travel on the team bus, but I couldn't care less. Kyle had a little bit of jet lag from the flight, but the culture shock was what got him immediately. The bus pulled over to the side of the Autobahn four hours into the trip, and my brother asked if everything was alright. I explained to him that this is where they switch Russian bus drivers. In Germany, bus and truck drivers can only drive for four hours straight before they legally have to take a break. Apparently, there was a bed under the bus where the backup driver would rest. These drivers were usually Russians who were in the country illegally. So when you looked out of the window halfway through the trip, the cargo door would open and a 50-year-old Russian would crawl out. Then the current driver of the bus would have a smoke, climb into the cargo area, and close the door. My brother watched this unfold in disbelief. We then drove for another two hours before pulling into a rest area. "Now what's going on?" my brother asked. "Kaffee und Kuchen," I replied. This was our mandatory coffee and cake stop outside, in the dead of winter. Players would slowly walk off of the bus to a nearby picnic table, where a trainer would lay out a spread of German pastries and coffee. The team would sit around in the cold and eat and drink for 15 minutes. After that, we loaded the bus and finished our drive. Kyle's first six hours in Germany were a whirlwind, but there was more to come.

The rink was an outdoor venue. Some German arenas were open ended, meaning the sides and top of the rink were covered but both ends were open, so there would be a stiff breeze during the game. I was never one for a hard warm-up but when we played in these rinks, I would wear a turtleneck, do four laps, take some shots, and get off immediately to warm myself in the dressing room. I'd be freezing my butt off, and some lunatic in the crowd would be shirtless, holding a tall glass of beer in one hand and a sparkler in the other. The German fans were wild. Kyle settled into the game and managed to order some drinks without knowing any German. After the game, buckets of beer were brought onto the bus for the ride home. Kyle realized that the bottles weren't twist off tops, so he asked, "Where is the bottle opener?" Much like when I asked the same question for the first time, he got a good laugh from the team. Latso proceeded to open his bottle with his teeth, Jaro opened his beer with a hockey stick, Janne opened his bottle on the overhead compartment, and I opened mine using another bottle. After seeing all of this, Kyle had a chuckle and learned to open a bottle the European way. By the end of the trip, he knew how to open bottles of beer without an opener and learned the phrases ein bier bitte, danke, and tschuss. As always, he had the time of his life.

During his visit, we took Kyle to visit Cologne. We had dinner in the city, walked around, and then headed home on the Autobahn. The weather was getting pretty bad, and we hit some traffic 30 minutes away from Neuwied. After an hour in terrible standstill traffic, we heard on the radio that they had closed the Autobahn for the night, and we weren't going to be moving anytime soon. I spent the next six hours trying to sleep, turning the car on and off to keep warm, and attempting to avoid the terrible gas coming out of my brother. People were going to the bathroom right in the middle of the highway, helicopters were flying overhead, and the whole experience was surreal. Apparently Germans don't plow the roads when the weather gets bad, they just close them and lock the cars onto the highway. We arrived home exhausted at 7 a.m.

The year was wrapping up and I was having a great season. Tyson was incredible to play with, I was receiving more than enough ice time, and I was making a lot of money. The euro to Canadian dollar exchange was awesome, and I never paid for a thing. The car was free, our apartment was free, and most of our meals were free. I just paid for gas and groceries. I was using $3,000 a month to pay off our student loans. I ended up finishing the season with 32 goals and 34 assists in 47 games, with 178 penalty minutes. I decided if I was going to play pro hockey and make money, I was going to be a meathead. I tried to hit everything that moved, I was cross-checking, fighting, and acting like a barbarian. The fans played the song "Wild Thing" whenever I got a penalty, and I didn't recognize who I was anymore. If I could score a goal, get two assists, and take a double minor for something stupid at the end of the game, I was happy. Jess would sit in the VIP lounge during the game and drink free wine while pretending to watch the game. Jess wasn't a big hockey fan and that's a big reason why I loved her. I didn't want to marry someone who knew the score of the Leafs game from the night before or who watched hockey on TV. A couple of times, I had to break it to her that the VIP lounge wasn't available for the game that night, and she opted to stay home instead.

At the end of the season, our coach, Fred Carroll, was in the hot seat. Germans love to fire their coaches and that seemed to be the discussion all season long. Fred was a great guy who spoke fluent German and treated me like a king. The team's ownership made it clear that if we lost our game in Schweinfurt, Fred was out. Frosty, who I played with at Western, was playing in Schweinfurt that season, and we had the opportunity to catch up after the game. It was always funny how paths crossed in hockey, and it proved what a small world it actually was. It was great to see him. As far as the game was concerned, there was absolutely no way that I was going to let Fred get fired. He was a great coach, and I liked having another Canadian around. I played one of the best games of my life, scoring a couple of goals and earning a bunch of assists, and we won easily. I can remember two games in my entire career when I felt like I was unstoppable and I could do whatever I wanted to on the ice. One of those games was in major bantam for Halton, in the playoffs against London. The other game was that night in Schweinfurt. Fred ended up keeping his job, and he finished the year with the team. More importantly, Schweinfurt had the most outrageous intermission entertainment that anyone had ever seen. Their team was sponsored by the local gentlemen's club. For the record, nudity and bare breasts meant nothing to Germans. Newspapers and magazines had nude photos on their front pages all the time, and the local video store had pornography right beside the new releases. After the first period ended in Schweinfurt, staff laid down towels at the red line. Two women sauntered onto the ice and proceeded to "entertain" the crowd for five minutes. It was right out of the movie *Slap Shot*, and something I hope to never experience again.

When we were finally eliminated from the playoffs, Jess and I couldn't wait to get home. It had been eight months since we left Canada, and we missed our family and friends. I learned a lot in my first year overseas, and I loved the town of Neuwied. I had great teammates, we had great fans, and Jess and I enjoyed each other's company. We must have bowled over 100 games that season, as Neuweid had this bowling alley that was owned by a man who was connected to the American army base nearby. The owner would bring Tyson chewing tobacco, Miller Genuine Draft, and other food items that we couldn't get in our small town. The bowling alley became our second home, and more importantly, it gave us something to do. At the end of every night, Jess and I would play cribbage and drink tea. She killed me in cribbage that season 65 games to 50, but I destroyed her in bowling. Let's just say, we had a lot of free time on our hands. I ended up renegotiating my contract with Neuwied for the next season, cutting Drago out of the deal. Drago was not happy with the Champ. To this day, I tell my kids that if they ever see a small, upset Slovenian man on the driveway, lock the front door. We flew home ready to spend some much-needed time with our families.

When Jessie and I returned to Canada, we set up shop in London for the summer. Jessie and I took supply teaching gigs until the end of the school year, and I mixed in my workouts in between. As I got older, I began dreading summer workouts. I had been working out for 14 summers in a row, trying to build strength and keep up my cardiovascular conditioning. Over time, these workouts become monotonous and it becomes difficult to get motivated to go to the gym. Essentially, it's like any other job, where you just don't want to go to work some days. The workouts usually lasted two to three hours a day, for four days a week. I hated running, and I will never ride another stationary bike for as long as I live. I didn't skate regularly until August, and I would ramp things up as the season got closer. By the end of my career, carrying my bag into the rink, getting dressed, and going through a conditioning skate was not a whole lot of fun. That is why Joe Thornton's 23 seasons in the NHL is so impressive. It's just not the grind of the regular season that's gruelling, it's also the summer training that goes with it. Training camp in Germany was extremely tough. We would skate in the morning, do extensive off-ice training in the afternoon, and return to the rink at night. I always thought I was in great shape until I arrived at German training camp. Europeans love their conditioning skate and off-ice workouts. As the season progressed, Mondays were our day off and we practiced twice on Tuesdays, along with a spin class in the morning. We had two practices on Wednesdays, with some dryland training mixed in. Thursday was a one-hour skate, and Friday was our weekend home game. The week was a grind because I was getting a ton of ice time, and we were still practicing up to six times a week. If I could've paid someone to tie and untie my skates before each ice time that season, I would have forked out the money as soon as possible. This was the point of my life that hockey became more of a job than a game, and I only enjoyed the perks that came with it.

We returned to Neuwied for my second season, in a new apartment closer to town. Janne, the Finnish import, lived downstairs with his wife and daughter. For the first half of the year, we would often hear Janne's wife yelling, "Ei, Janne!" We just figured that Finns were like their Canadian counterparts and said eh before or after each sentence. By Christmas, we learned that ei meant no in Finnish, and that his wife spent half of her life, yelling, "No, Janne." On weekends after games, Janne would sneak upstairs to our apartment for four of his favourite things in life: cards, beer, chew, and Sean Paul. Janne and Tiina became good friends, and I learned that Finns are as close to being Canadian as you can get in this world. I also learned that cheering for Sweden in any sport is forbidden.

That summer, Jess and I found out that she was pregnant with our first child. It was an exciting time but nerve-wracking as well. We were going to be in Germany for the due date, away from family and friends. Early in the year, we were set up with a German midwife named Dorothie, and she was absolutely perfect. Dorothie spoke enough broken English to communicate with us, and her experience and capability put us at ease. Communicating was always difficult in Neuwied, as very few people spoke any English at all. During one of our routine checkups at the Krankenhaus, the nurse was searching for our baby's heartbeat. She was startled suddenly and had a panicked look on her face. Jess asked her in German if everything was alright, and she struggled to say, "No heartbeat," in English. This put Jessie into an immediate panic, and the nurse, who was struggling with her English, ran out of the room to get a doctor. The doctor ended up explaining to us that the nurse was, "Having trouble finding a heartbeat, but everything was okay." From then on, we brought Dorothie to all of our doctor's appointments. Jessie didn't want to know the sex of the baby until the birth. I'm not good with surprises, so I needed to know what we were having. I had found out the sex of the baby at a doctor's appointment in Canada before we left for Germany, but nobody else knew anything. I spent the remaining seven months tormenting grandparents, siblings, and Jess with accidental slips of "he" or "she," and I told some people that we were having a girl and others that it was going to be a boy.

One of the clauses in my contract with Neuwied was that the team would pay for Jess to go to school to learn German. She attended the Volksschule in town on Tuesday nights, so at least one of us would understand what was happening around us. What Jess wasn't expecting was that she was going to be the only woman in the class who wasn't a mail-order bride. There were women from Russia, Turkey, and South America in her class. Their plane would land in Germany, and they would meet their husbands at the airport. The German men would pick the women out of a catalogue and pay a fee to marry them in Germany. Of course, Jess became friends with all of these women and would share their emotional stories with me when she came home from class. She looked forward to going to class each Tuesday night and hanging out with her new international friends. Jess loves learning new languages, and she added German to her repertoire of Spanish and French.

Jess's ability to speak different languages was a huge asset for us as we travelled around Europe. My German, on the other hand, consisted of phrases I picked up at the arena, the sandwich shop, the grocery store, and by watching MTV. German television was hilarious. On their sports channel at 8 p.m., you would be watching a Bundesliga soccer game with FC Bayern Munich. After the game ended, there would be a woman on the screen swinging a golf club, playing bocce, or kicking a soccer ball while stripping. They called it *Sexy Sport Clips*. I'd have to explain to Jess that I was just watching a soccer game. Nudity was definitely an expression of freedom and personal development in Germany.

Our hockey team had its own tradition every Tuesday night as well. We had what was called Kabinefest, and it was a team get-together in the bottom of a house. The basement had long wooden tables, a fully stocked bar with German beer, a lot of music, and we ordered a ton of food to be delivered in. It felt like a mini Oktoberfest. Upstairs, there were saunas and showers for us to unwind in and physio tables to get treatment on. You would have two beers, jump in the sauna, and then come out to get your hip flexor worked on by an intoxicated German physiotherapist eating a ham sandwich. We would roam around the house for hours, circulating between the sauna, playing cards, eating, and having a couple of drinks. It was something I looked forward to each week, and it was a German hockey tradition.

Our team had this trainer who looked like Albert Einstein and rode around town on a bicycle. He was always three sheets to the wind, and he talked non-stop. In retrospect, some of my junior hockey trainers were neurosurgeons compared to him. He would get absolutely plastered at Kabinefest every Tuesday, somehow ride his bike home, and show up to the rink the next day to do his job, as if nothing had ever happened. His name was Ecky, and he was definitely not qualified to treat an injury or to even hand a hockey stick to a player. He was a cheap trainer option that could fill water bottles and make great coffee. We didn't care who the trainer was in Neuwied, as it saved more money for our contracts and our trainer didn't sharpen skates anyways. Our captain, Jens, sharpened the skates. If you ever lost an edge during the game, you'd tell Jens you lost an edge and needed your skates sharpened. Jens would tell the coach he couldn't go on next and would take the skate and disappear down the tunnel. We would send out another centre with his line, and when Jens returned with the skate, his line would be back up at the door. He billed the team each time he sharpened the skates. If you ever broke a holder on your skate, Jens would be gone for an entire period, leaving the team down two players in the process. When I first arrived in Germany, I was in shock that this was the system, but by the end of my time with the team, I figured I was making Jens some money.

Our team hired a Czech coach for the second season, as Fred received a better contract from another team. Our new coach didn't speak a single word of English except for Joosteen and fitness. I can still hear him in my head yelling for me to come off the ice screaming, "Joosteen, auf gehts!" I pretended that I couldn't understand a single word of German all season, and it frustrated him to no end. Come off the ice? Nicht verstanden. Back check? Nicht verstanden. Sit back in a trap? Nicht verstanden. Don't slash a guy over the back? Nicht verstanden. I went on the ice whenever I wanted and played however I wanted. The greatest part of German Eishockey was that you could have two goals and three assists, be a -2, and the fans would name you the player of the game. Imports were meant to score, not to defend. The new coach loved fitness. Everything was conditioning, and I felt like I was training for the Munich Olympics in '72. If there was a half marathon or calisthenics competition during the mid-season break, I was ready for action.

Each year, there was a four-day break in the middle of the season that acted like an all-star break. Jessie and I googled various cities and then took off for a couple of days in the Mitsubishi. We travelled to Amsterdam, Paris, Brugge, Austria, and every part of Germany that we could get to. We never booked a hotel or made any real plans, we just flew by the seat of our pants. Our first season, after visiting Paris for two days, we took the long way back to Germany, down the beaches of Normandy. I was always fascinated with Canadian history, and it was on the top of my bucket list to see the French beaches with my own eyes. We pulled into Juno Beach and there wasn't a single person anywhere. I stood on the beach for an hour, staring at the water and imagining what it would have been like to storm Juno Beach on D-Day. It was a very clear day and I could see for miles around me. It was unbelievable to imagine what the Canadian troops were walking into that day and the courage that was involved. Jessie and I headed to the Canadian War Memorial in town, and we walked around in silence for over an hour. It was emotional reading the tombstones, looking at the Canadian flags, and seeing the impeccable conditions the grounds were kept in after all of these years. You feel patriotic and thankful to see an unknown teenager's name, with his age of 17 etched into the stone. It's an eerie feeling when you recognize a town that is close to your hometown on the white headstone. It was an experience I'll never forget, and it makes you think about how small the game of hockey is compared to everything else going on in the world. Some people dedicate their entire lives to finding a better breakout, designing power play systems, playing mind games with their players, and developing a God complex. Meanwhile, there are people trying to cure cancer and soldiers who gave up their lives for our freedom, and we don't ever talk about them except for one day in November. People know the stats of Wayne Gretzky's 1989 season or the average puck possession time for the Toronto Maple Leafs, but they choose to ignore these young soldiers laying in a field off the shores of Juno Beach. It humbles you very quickly and puts the fact that you dedicated half of your life to a game into a different perspective.

Early in January of that second year, Joshua James Mortimer Davis was born. The labour was very quick, and he was born healthy in Neuwied,

Germany, on January 24. I will never forget being distracted during Jess's delivery by the angry German women screaming at the top of their lungs in delivery rooms nearby. Labour is definitely more frightening when the screams are in German, so anything Jessie screamed seemed like it was coming from an angel. Dorothie made the process very easy, and there weren't any issues with the hospital. I was very familiar with the Neuwied hospital because I had been admitted with severe pneumonia that same season. I was put into a shared room with two elderly German men who seemed like they were straight out of a movie. They would wake up first thing in the morning and complain about how hungry they were. When the nurses arrived, they would ask what was taking so long for breakfast to be served. Breakfast would eventually arrive, and all I would hear is "Scheisse Frühstück," meaning the breakfast was crap. The dynamic duo would then fall asleep immediately, like they had severe narcolepsy. After their snore-filled nap was over, the two of them would start moaning that lunch was late once again. When lunch would arrive, actually on time, these two would complain, "scheisse Mittagessen," which essentially meant "crappy lunch." At the time, I felt like these two men were making fun of me as I lay there, but I would just smile and nod my head. This went on for three days, and I felt like I was in the German version of *Grumpy Old Men*. At the end of it, I was begging to come home.

I finished my second year in Neuwied in a unique situation, to say the least. In mid-December, I received one of my paycheques a week late. When the following paycheque didn't come at all, I knew there was an issue. We had a team meeting with the president of the team because, as I mentioned before, teams did not have an owner. Through what I could understand of his broken English and through discussions with my teammates, I realized we were in financial trouble. Two of the company sponsors were not having a successful year and they could not pay the rest of their sponsorship money. When you are short $400,000 of your budget, it's not easy to make up that shortfall. By the middle of January, I was told that we were "insolvent," or bankrupt. I wasn't going to receive another paycheque that season, and I was in a complete panic. The other players seemed comfortable with this, as it supposedly happens all the time in Germany. A team will go bankrupt and will have to slide down to the lowest league to start over. If your team name was SCM Neuwied, your new team name becomes Neuwied EC. The team spends a couple of years trying to get promoted and will eventually end up in the same league, with a new name, new jerseys and new players. This was news to me and my stress level was through the roof.

Our team met with an insolvency lawyer and he laid out the plans for the months to come. We would continue playing, and the government would reimburse us for the money we didn't receive after the season was over. Basically, I had to continue to play hockey in order to get paid for the four months that the team wasn't going to be paying me. I wouldn't receive a paycheque in January, February, March, and April, but I would hopefully receive a lump sum in June from the German government. I had to continue playing hockey like nothing was happening, with the knowledge that this team was going to fold next season, and hope that 14,000 euros ($20,000 Canadian) would eventually end up in my Canadian bank account. I couldn't understand what the lawyer was saying and all of the documents were in German. If I ever had to have blind faith, this was the time.

Josh changed our lives a lot. We didn't have a crib or any baby items for him, so Josh slept on an ottoman next to our bed. I would dangle the keys to the Mitsubishi over his head for entertainment, so if he ever buys a Lancer, we'll know why. Jess's mom was the only family member to come visit us, and it was nice to have her help for the week. It was always tough for Jess, as I was continuing to play hockey. I finished the year with 25 goals and 26 assists for 51 points. Tyson was on another team that season, so points were harder to come by. He ended up receiving his German pass (given to foreign players who qualify for German citizenship so they no longer count as an import) years later and played in the top league in Germany. Our team was in the middle of the pack — exactly what the board of directors wanted. The group of guys was essentially the same but with a few new additions. We added Oleg Tokarev, a defenceman from Russia. He disappeared for two weeks during the season without telling anyone and arrived back at practice like nothing had happened. When I asked where he had been, he replied, "I had business." I still liked hockey, but with Fred and Tyson gone and Josh in the picture, I was ready to go home. It was tough having a baby without any family nearby and without being unable to share these special moments with your friends. We were updating everyone back home through a blog, but it wasn't the same as being there in person. When we arrived home three months after Josh was born, it was the first time everyone got to meet him. It was an exciting moment at the airport, and Jess and I were happy to be home.

Months later, the money finally arrived. It was a huge relief for us, as we didn't have a single dollar left to our name. We used every last penny during those four months in Germany, and we even managed to travel to Florence after the season was over. We loaded Josh onto the plane and carried him in a Baby Bjorn as we travelled around Italy. Josh ended up clearing out a couple of hotels on the trip with his late night crying. We would run through the lobby the next morning with him hidden under our coat so people wouldn't know that we were "that couple." When we finally arrived back at our apartment in London, Ontario, I started my training once again. One morning I went out for a short jog before work, and I stopped the run six minutes in. I walked along the Thames River back to the apartment and told Jess I was done. My passion for training and my love of the game was gone. I loved everything that went along with the game of hockey, but I couldn't play it anymore. I had a young son and a degree, and I was ready to move on. Jess would've loved to go back overseas for a couple more years, but I couldn't do it anymore. It's impossible to play professional hockey and to perform at your highest level if you hate the game. This moment finally came to me at 28 years old. I was officially retiring.

CHAPTER 10
FAMILY, TEACHING, AND THE END OF THE ROAD
(Dundas Real McCoys, 2007–14)

In 2006, Jess and I were hired to teach in Guelph, Ontario. We were busy like any young family, and I had no desire whatsoever to play hockey. When you arrive in a new city and people hear that you played professional hockey, they always want you to play on their men's league team. I was dodging invites from people for the first couple of months, and I would have to explain to them that I hated the game. I would constantly get a raised eyebrow and a confused look from people as they would ask me why. My answer was always the same, if you did something every day for 14 years, excluding minor hockey, would you be in a rush to play again? Finally, after four months of dodging invites, I was dragged out to a men's league game at 10:30 p.m. It was the Guelph Men's "A" league, and I knew right away that this wasn't a good fit for me. I seemed to be the only guy on the ice who realized that it was Tuesday night at 10:30 p.m. and that the

Albion Hotel was the crest on the front of our jerseys. Guys were hacking and slashing all over the ice, and when I returned to the bench after a shift, a young kid told me I needed to backcheck harder. I explained to him that it was 10:45 p.m., and I wouldn't be backchecking any harder for the rest of the evening. You realize very quickly that men's league hockey is a place for "AA" level hockey players to try as hard as they can. Women are in the crowd watching their boyfriends play, and I'd laugh, as I couldn't even get my wife to watch me play professional hockey. When these tryhards locked in on someone who once played a high level of hockey, it was like shark bait. This was their big opportunity to see if they could have ever played pro, and they want to tell their friends later that night that they were way better than the former professional player on the ice. Meanwhile, I'm just trying to get a sweat in, trying not to get hurt for work the next day, and looking forward to wings after the game. I retired after that one game, and I will never play men's league hockey ever again.

Later on that year, I got a call to play senior hockey in Tillsonburg, Ontario. I told the GM absolutely no way would I play, but thanks for calling. He asked what it would take for me to sign, and I brilliantly said new skates, four sticks, and $100 a game. Surprisingly he said that would be fine, and I reluctantly became a Tillsonburg Viper. I played eight games during that season, and I actually didn't play too badly. I still liked the competition aspect of the game and the league had some pretty good players. Nobody was doing anything stupid on the ice, and it was much different than the men's league hockey from a couple months before. The next year, I was asked to play again in Tillsonburg, but I declined, as the drive was just too far. Besides, I now had my new skates and enough sticks to keep me happy for a while.

In 2007, I couldn't find a teaching job in Guelph, so I stayed home with Josh. Looking back on it, it was a great experience, but I needed to find something to do at night. I could only participate in so many play dates and mommy and me classes before I lost my mind. When I was teaching at Centennial Collegiate the previous year, I volunteered to help coach the girls hockey team. I loved working with the girls team, and by the end of the season I had taken over as the head coach. We had an amazing group of girls, and five of them went on to play Canadian university hockey. The girls listened to everything I had to say, and they wanted to learn and get better. It quietly brought back some of my passion for the game. I had the opportunity to show them how to play the game correctly, I could run a structured practice, and more importantly, I could make hockey fun. My goal was to make each day enjoyable for the girls, and I wanted them to find their joy in hockey. I stopped coaching the team when my contract was up at Centennial, but a part of me still missed the game. So when I transitioned into a stay-at-home dad who had nothing to do at night, I opened up to the possibility of playing hockey once again.

My phone rang and it was 1994 all over again. "JD, it's Spud, I was wondering if you wanted to come play senior hockey in Dundas." I hadn't seen Spud since my Junior B days in Cambridge, but he was now coaching the Dundas Real McCoys in the Ontario Hockey Association's Major League Hockey. I asked Spud what the team could offer me, and he said, "Gas money, cold beer, and some good stories." I had a good laugh and I told him that I was in. Dundas was a blast. We had a great group of players to start with, and much like Western, the team was built from there. Ryan Christie and Nick Smith were two former NHLers, and they formed a nucleus for the group going forward. Friends would contact friends, and we eventually had a great team. Most of all, it was an incredible dressing room. By the time I finished playing in Dundas, I had played with Todd Harvey, Todd Hlushko, Matthew Barnaby, Jay McKee, and a many others who had played in the NHL or in top leagues across the world. What we all had in common was that we missed the competition and, most of all, we missed the dressing room. You may be asking, If you hated hockey so much and your junior career was so traumatic, why did you play for 14 more years? Easy, the dressing room. Our owner, Don Robertson never paid the under-the-table salaries that the other teams in the league did. He realized very early on that if he could keep the guys happy in the dressing room after games and practices, they would play for Dundas for a very long time. The team had a beer fridge, everyone had their own stall, and sticks were free. Tape was provided, we had real certified trainers, and the trainers would pack your bag for road games and bring it to the arena. It's a huge plus when you don't have to pack your bag and you can feel like a professional hockey player. It's a simple thing, but we were simple people. More importantly, there were discounted wings at the Collins after each game. What Don realized was that it wasn't the game that we all missed, it was the camaraderie that came with it.

The dressing room in Dundas was like nothing I'd experienced before. That was saying something, as I had been in some pretty good rooms throughout my career. Dundas was a combination of all of those dressing rooms but on steroids. You would take a deep breath outside before entering the room each week because most of the team would be sitting in their stall, waiting for the next person to walk in. They would make fun of your shirt, your jeans, your shoes, your haircut, the way you walked or anything that you said. I loved it. We joked that if we said any of these things to a civilian at work, they would end up in the fetal position in the corner of the office. These were some of the funniest teammates I had ever played with. and it was over 300 years of pro hockey stories combined in one dressing room. Stories from the NHL, AHL, ECHL, Europe, and the OHL lasted for hours each night. Guys would have a couple of drinks, sit back, and enjoy the show. It was a break from your everyday life, and for me, it was a break from being a dad. One night, a guy came back into the dressing room because he forgot his truck keys. While he was getting the keys from his stall, he sat down and started listening to the story being told. Two hours later there was a knock on the door. A woman was looking for the guy who came back to get his keys. The guy who answered the door yelled, "Hey, I think your girlfriend wants to get going, she's said she's been waiting outside for two hours." This was normal in Dundas, but who could leave during a good story?

I ended playing for the Real McCoys for seven years. The core guys stayed around, much like university, and we added different pieces each year. I was lucky enough to play in four Allan Cups over my seven years in Dundas. During that time, I had the opportunity to play in some world-class cities, such as Brantford, Ontario; Steinbach, Manitoba; Fort St. John,

B.C.; and Kenora, Ontario. We should have won some of those tournaments, but our team didn't travel well. The average age was 30 years old, but when we got on the road, the team turned into a bunch of 16-year-olds. We would have a team meeting at the hotel each year and talk about how this was going to be the year that we were going to take the tournament very seriously. Then, two hours later, half of the team would be missing, and they would show up 24 hours later. We would cross our fingers and hope that everyone made it to the bus the next day. In my last season with Dundas, we won the bid to host the 2014 Allan Cup. Our team was extremely focused on winning that year, and we were confident that we weren't going to throw this championship away. The tournament was in Dundas, so nobody could disappear, and the team was safe from any other stupidity. For most of us, we quietly knew that this was the end of the road. It was becoming too much of a grind to balance hockey with work and family. I was coaching my high school hockey team in Orangeville and my son's Atom AAA team in Guelph. I started working with the Guelph Storm, and I was still teaching while trying to be a dad to three kids. Playing hockey was no longer an option for me after this season.

It was a great opportunity to play in Dundas for my last Allan Cup. The kids were able to watch me play, and my friends and family were close by. As always, my brother, Kyle, spent a lot of time with the team and he was a fixture in the dressing room. My best friend Neal from Carlisle and Kyle saw more games in more cities than anyone other than my parents. Don Robertson made the Allan Cup a family affair. For the first game, he allowed our kids to dress in a Dundas jersey and stand with us on the blueline for "O Canada." I had my best tournament out of any of the Allan Cups I played in, and it felt great. Our team was clicking, and we easily advanced to the championship game against the Clarenville Caribou. I knew that this was going to be my last hockey game ever, so the drive to the rink was surreal. I was reflecting back on all of my great hockey memories, and I was excited that I got to finish my career on my terms. All of these years later, I would play my last game in a building where I played minor hockey and started my career in Junior C. My life had definitely come full circle. My wife and kids would be in the crowd and my parents would get to see my last game. My mom and dad had been through a lot with me, so I was happy that they were going to be there to take it all in. Dundas played in a great old rink that was perfect for senior hockey. The arena was packed with standing room only for the final game and it was an amazing atmosphere. The Allan Cup final was televised on TSN, so my students, friends, and family could all watch the game at home. Regulation ended in a 2–2 tie and, of course, we were headed to overtime. This was my third national championship game, and third national championship overtime. I was hoping my luck wouldn't finally run out, and I could sneak in one more overtime win. Early in the first frame, I won a faceoff in the offensive zone, and Randy Rowe buried the one-timer into the top corner past the Clarenville goaltender. We won.

I had won my third major Canadian hockey trophy, and the arena went crazy. First awarded in 1909, the Allan Cup is the oldest trophy of the three championships I had won. The trophy was presented live on TSN, and Jess and the kids came onto the ice for photos. I will never forget that afternoon in Dundas, and I was lucky enough to win my last hockey game. A couple of months after the tournament, our family got some time with the trophy. In keeping with tradition, the Allan Cup accidentally broke into two pieces at our house. I handed the 105-year-old trophy back to our assistant coach the next day with the cup in my left hand and the rest of it in my right. I said to him with a straight face, "I think it needs to be welded back together, Bernie." He was not pleased. You can barely see the weld on the trophy at the Hockey Hall of Fame — believe me, I had a look. I ended up playing in 151 games with Dundas over those seven seasons, and I had 122 goals, 173 assists, and 295 points. Not a bad finish for someone who never thought he'd play after retiring from professional hockey years earlier. Best of all, I left the game a winner and on my own terms. Not bad for a kid from Flamborough Minor Hockey.

CHAPTER 11

LOOSE ENDS AND A STEP TO THE FUTURE

So when I started this exercise of unpacking my feelings, I assumed it would be 20 pages of my thoughts on the game of hockey and a brief look at the role that it played in my life. I wanted to acknowledge the skills and tools that I acquired in my lifelong hockey journey, as well as the positive growth I experienced. Similarly, I wanted to examine my life's struggles and explore why my body feels the way it does. I wanted to wrestle with some of the anxieties that I face daily, the constant challenges that I feel with irritability, and my frequent episodes of dizziness. Lastly, I wanted to discover if everything I sacrificed mentally, socially, and physically was worth winning championships and being drafted to the NHL. Would I do it all over again? Do I want my own kids to go through the same process? The writing stirred up great memories from my past and it also became therapeutic. My story is not from the perspective of a player who won two Stanley Cups, had a 10-year pro career, and made millions of dollars. My journey is the story of thousands of kids who were chasing a dream and ended up playing all over the world. This is the story that kids and parents need to hear, not the tale of the privileged career of an NHL superstar born with rare talent. My journey is a story of resilience, injury, depression, friendship, strength, family, and the future. It's a story of a "thousandaire" who chased his hockey dream. So what has happened since I retired from the game and what does my future hold? Where do I start?

Injuries affect all of us in the game, but we never really feel the effects until we get much older. My career doesn't compare to someone who fought in the minor leagues for 10 seasons or an NHL player who played a physical style for their entire career. I stood in front of the net and took a pounding, I didn't shy away from the dangerous areas on the ice, and I wasn't afraid to fight once in a while. That said, I wasn't putting my body on the line each and every night. I worked as hard as I could most of the time and suffered a veritable laundry list of injuries:

Flamborough Junior C — Minor concussion, left shoulder separation
Cambridge Junior B — Minor concussion, right shoulder separation, left tibial tuberosity fracture
Kingston Frontenacs OHL — Major concussion, two minor concussions, 15 stitches in my lip, three stitches in my chin, fractured thumb
Soo Greyhounds OHL — Major concussion (ICU), minor concussion, five stitches in my lip
Ottawa 67's OHL — Separated left shoulder, minor concussion, six stitches in my eyebrow, torn groin, two broken ribs, fractured foot
Western Mustangs — Separated right shoulder, two minor concussions, four stitches on my wrist
SCM Neuwied (Germany) — Minor concussion, four stitches on my chin, broken nose, thumb contusion
Dundas Real McCoys — two minor concussions, five stitches under my eye, broken sternum

So what do I remember the most out of all of these injuries? The thumb contusion in Germany was just a hard slash on my thumb, but it was brutal. The swelling was so bad that later that night, it became too painful to sleep. I couldn't take it anymore. I woke up in the middle of the night, I took a picture off of our wall, and I removed the metal nail behind it. I heated the end of the nail on the burner of the stove and started grinding it into my fingernail. I eventually put the metal nail through my fingernail into my thumb and it caused an explosion of blood. Jess was horrified and told me I needed a tetanus shot, but I slept like a baby. The high stick in Dundas missed my eyeball by a millimetre, the broken nose was awful, the tibial fracture left me immobilized for five weeks, and the wrist stitches from a skate only missed a major tendon by a centimetre. The broken sternum was terrible, the groin tear caused a lot of issues later on, and the majority of my face stitches were from being a below average fighter. What defines a minor concussion? My definition was anything that didn't cause a loss of memory or consciousness. I now have trouble sleeping on either shoulder because of the numerous separations, and I can't raise my arms over my head. Both of the bones on my elbows are completely chipped off, so I can't lean on a table or the bone moves up my arm. Let's just say elbow pads were not custom fit in my time. I now have two herniated discs in my back that caused me to miss three months of work, and I battle dizziness if things are moving too fast around me. My feet are deformed after wearing skates every day, and my jaw locks if I open it too wide. Other than that, I'm good.

On the mental side, there have been a lot of repercussions. I panic if I think I'm going to be late for anything and setting my alarm clock is like solving a Rubik's cube. I check it, I recheck it, and then I check it again. My OCD isn't visible, but if you watch me long enough, you'll notice the trends. I have to do everything in threes and if it doesn't feel right, I reset and do it again. If I kiss my daughter on the head, I kiss her three times.

If I check my alarm clock, it's checked three times. Sips of water before I go to bed? Three sips. I put everything on left to right, and if I forget, I reset and start again. Left sock, then right sock. Left skate, then right skate. Left arm in a jacket, then right arm in a jacket. If I leave the house, I will always have to go back in because I have to make sure the stove is off, the lights are off, or the front door is locked. Jess's favourite is my sniffing before I go to bed. I sniff multiple times until I feel like everything is clear and I'm ready to sleep. If it becomes too much, Jess will say, "Reset and go to sleep."

What causes all of this? Well, where do I begin? Let me take you through a typical game day on the road. Breakfast is from 9 to 9:30 a.m., The bus leaves for pregame skate at 9:45 a.m., but that actually means 9:40 and you can't miss breakfast. You have to be on the ice at 10:27 for the 10:30 skate. The skate is over at 11:00 and the bus leaves for the hotel at 11:45. Again, the bus actually leaves at 11:40. Pregame meal is at 12:30 p.m., so the bus leaves at 12:20, but really the bus leaves at 12:15. You return to the hotel from the pregame meal at 1:30 and the bus leaves for the actual game at 5:30. Guys will usually nap, so that means setting your alarm or getting a wakeup call for 4:30. After waking up, you take a shower, get dressed, and grab a coffee. The bus actually leaves at 5:25, not 5:30. The team meeting at the rink is at 6:00 and then you get a five-minute warning for warm-up at 6:50. The team takes the ice at 6:55 and warm-up is 20 minutes long, but you can get off at the 17-minute mark. The coach comes in at 7:23 and you leave the tunnel at 7:28. The warm-up laps before the anthem last for two minutes. "O Canada" is sung and the puck is dropped. After the game, you can meet with any family or friends at the game, and you are then given a two-minute warning when the bus is leaving. Pretty simple, right? This is an example of one day on the road, and probably what triggered my OCD.

Most of the days are good days, and I feel relatively healthy for my age. My back has improved thanks to a fantastic osteopath and a 40-minute daily stretching and core exercise routine. If I had trained and maintained my body specifically like this earlier in my life, I know I would have been a better hockey player. I understand that I played in a different generation.

I still get bad headaches, I feel anxious in public, and I occasionally get confused and forget where I'm going. My hands often feel shaky, I have bigger mood swings than before, and I get dizzy when I rotate 180 degrees in a busy space. I struggle to feel emotion, especially sadness in sentimental moments. Most of all, I'm angry. I can't fathom that I wasn't given the proper medical care at the junior level, with the exception of the trainer in Sault Ste. Marie, who quite possibly saved my life. That one trained professional prevented the bus from driving any farther with me in the condition that I was in. I'm angry that the Kingston Frontenacs threw me into a dark shower as a Band-Aid for a major head injury — I'm angry that the game took priority. I'm angry that the management in the Soo desperately tried to save money at the expense of a severely injured player, and I'm angry that nobody advocated for me, except for my parents and one of my agents. I'm terrified of what lies ahead, but I try to remain optimistic. Maybe some of what I'm feeling is a result of getting older. My body has a lot of wear and tear, and these could be the natural repercussions of those injuries. I can deal with the physical pain of my body, but it's the impact of my head injuries that worries me the most. One day we will find out, but I'm anxious about the potential implications it will have on my family.

There are many times I wish I hadn't gone through everything that I did. Don't get me wrong, hockey was very good to me and I can't ignore the positives that the game has provided for me. That is why sifting through my experiences and figuring out what really happened to me has been so difficult. I don't want to complain. I owe much of who I am today to hockey, but recently, the negative impacts have taken centre stage. The game has had an enormous impact on me physically and mentally, and I wish that I lived at home a bit longer, matured on my own, and spent more time with my family and friends. I missed out on a lot of things, but that was my choice and my parents always allowed me to make my own decisions, much like I do today with my own kids. That is why I value the opportunity to spend time with my kids and why I want sports to be a positive influence on their lives. Bobby Orr said it best: "Kids play far too much. Kids are playing twelve months a year — little ones. They don't need it. Play other sports. Have other coaches. Hang out with other kids, other parents. I think that's all healthy. Parents think their kids have to play for people to see them. Look, if your kid can play, they will find you." That's the advice that I choose to follow; the only problem is the other parents who get in the way. They have their own ideas on how to elevate their kids to future stardom.

So what about hockey? What's my relationship with the game that caused all of this pain? The experience of working with the girls hockey team at Centennial Collegiate Secondary School invigorated me, and it introduced me to the role of coaching. When I received my first contract teaching job at Orangeville District Secondary School, I wanted to build the boys hockey program into something special. I wanted to the team to feel like a family and to help kids be successful in both school and in life. Our program has been to the Ontario Federation of School Athletic Associations (OFSAA) championship three times in my 12 years coaching, and we have succeeded in winning our league six of these 12 years. I've had the opportunity to coach some great hockey players, and I've made a difference in their lives. I love to teach kids how to play the game well, how to play within a system that encourages offence and creativity, and how to play for your team. We play 2 Puck after each win, we save the last 10 minutes of each practice for fun, and I try to make everyone feel valued, even the player getting three shifts a game. It's fantastic when former players stop in for lunch or check in to see how I'm doing. I want the Orangeville Bears experience to be something they remember for the rest of their lives, much like some of the best teams that I played on. I have taken a little something from each coach that I ever played for, even the bad ones. I make a point to never treat anyone the way I was treated in the Soo and to positively engage with my players, like Spud and Brian Kilrea did. I'm thankful that I've had the opportunity to rediscover my passion for the game through this program.

I also had the opportunity to coach my son's Guelph AAA hockey teams from Novice to Pee Wee. I attempted to apply the same coaching techniques and ideas as my high school team, but one thing was always different: the parents. In high school hockey, it's the kids on the bus and in the dressing room, and the parents show up only for the games. They are thankful for the opportunity and the experience that their kids are receiving. In minor hockey, the parents continue to ruin the game. For the most part, we had a great group of parents in Guelph, but people put their own goals and dreams ahead of their children's. Early morning skills sessions, spring hockey, judging each practice from the glass, and constant negativity masked as feedback in the car ride home, suggesting that their coach is wrong, is all affecting their kids. If you have had three bad coaches in three years, do you think it's possible that the coaches aren't the issue — it's you? I've had moms tell me that we should put three forwards out on the penalty kill because the defencemen are the ones taking all the penalties and the forwards end up paying the price. *What?* I've had people suggest different monthly linemate combinations for their son for over a year, until they end up suggesting the same kid they didn't want their son to play with in the first place. Parents can be brutal. I spent hours planning my practices, rolled the lines evenly, provided extra development, and always finished practice with fun. We joked around in the dressing room, and I frequently organized team outings to keep everyone connected and on the same page. Remember, I was volunteering my own time and spending out of my own pocket. I even cut kids face to face with their parents in the room, so they would know why they didn't make the team and what to work on for next year. I didn't want young kids to have to look at a list and always wonder why they didn't make the team like my experience in Milton Junior A.

I knew from my own career that minor hockey should be the best period of time for a player. It wasn't my job to create NHLers or to develop the most-skilled individuals. I had the opportunity to teach the game, make the kids better hockey players, and keep hockey fun. Deep down, I wanted to recreate the setting of nine-year-old me jogging with my hockey bag to play shinny, just so I could get some more time on the ice. I wanted to see that same joy on the faces of my players. Most of all, I wanted to create lasting memories of good times playing hockey.

I've also had the privilege to work with the Guelph Storm over the past nine seasons. I was asked to volunteer as the team chaplain in 2012 and to provide mentorship to their players. I am a Christian and faith has always been an important part of my life. In the years that I struggled the most in hockey, I distanced myself from God and relied on myself. When I eventually realized that I couldn't control everything and that my life had a purpose, things changed for the better. I continue to tell players that everything happens for a reason and only God knows why certain things happen. Players voluntarily come to chapel, ask questions, and explore life outside of the game.

Years ago, a player took his own life in the OHL, and the league wanted to do everything they could to prevent this from ever happening again. Each team was encouraged to hire someone the players could talk to and receive support from, especially in times of crisis. This person would be independent of the coaching staff and management to secure player privacy. I could relate easily, as I was that same kid sitting in his bedroom in the Soo, depressed and isolated, wondering what I was doing with my life. I was excited to take on this role, as I knew from experience what these players were going through. My other role as chaplain is to help the players realize that hockey doesn't have to define them. Faith in something greater than yourself can help you appreciate that you cannot control everything, and you have to trust that your life has purpose and meaning no matter what. Why did I experience everything that I did over the course of my life? I feel like it was leading me to this position with the Storm. I can relate to anything the players are going through, and I can listen to their issues without passing judgment. I don't care if they ever make the NHL, I just want them to get through this process, feeling heard and understood. It's my goal every OHL season to take each player out for lunch and get to know them on a personal level. Over their four years with the team, I hope to develop a friendship and build enough trust between us that they know they can come to me for advice at any time. I've been lucky enough to have some great relationships over the years. Hopefully, those who need help reach out when they need it. After all, if I've learned one thing in my career, it's that hockey is only a game.

As part of the research for writing this book, I reached out to former teammates and friends to see if what I remember actually happened. Joe Thornton, World Junior gold medalist, Olympic gold medalist, and future Hall of Famer with a 22-year career in the NHL, returned my text immediately, like we were 18 years old again. Why was I nervous that he would even remember me? We retold old stories, joked about the OHL being the second best league in the world, and he made me feel like I mattered in the hockey world. Brian Campbell, Lady Byng recipient, Stanley Cup champion with 17 years in the NHL, asked how he could help in sharing my story, and we picked up right where we left off. Allan Walsh asked how I was doing; Jeff Hunt laughed at old stories. Every person I contacted was excited to hear how my life was going. Judy Kilrea picked up the phone and genuinely asked about my family before calling Brian to their landline like it was 1999 all over again. Brian Kilrea still cares about me and he spent the phone call telling me how important I was to his team in Ottawa, before he had to excuse himself to walk his dog. It all finally brought me to tears one day, to know that I hadn't imagined it and that I actually lived this life. My stories were true and my memory of the past hadn't faded away quite yet. Teammates appreciated me and I had an impact on the game of hockey. Telling other my story is the next step, and I hope I can continue to spark conversations as hockey evolves into its next chapter. I'm beginning to see my purpose and I am thankful for those who helped me along the way.

So if I was to ever play hockey again, what would it look like? I thought about that, and decided the league I play with must include:

1) icetime before 8:30 p.m.
2) former junior or pro players who understand the dream is over
3) good conversations in the room
4) a quick beverage

5) competitiveness but nothing over the top
6) a place to leave my bag afterwards

I was lucky enough to find a league like this over the past year, and I get to play once in a while. I actually get nervous going out to play because I'm at an age where I don't want to embarrass myself. I'm having fun, and I can still see the game in front of me, even if I can't get there as fast as I used to. It's funny playing with these younger guys and watching the current OHL. Players are so skilled and so much faster than we ever were. They play the game year round, they prepare properly off the ice, and they have special diets in place. Most high-level players have a skills coach, a shooting coach, and a power skating instructor. They are definitely more talented, but the players have become robots without the ability to see the entire ice. The on-ice vision and overall hockey sense of today's younger players has greatly diminished. The elite players are the ones who can see the game at a high pace while maintaining their overall skill. So why is hockey sense missing? I think it's because most kids play only one sport all year. It was normal for me to play baseball, soccer, basketball, and flag football in organized leagues. Playing other sports allowed me to adapt to different strategies and to see the game of hockey differently. I currently work with great hockey players who cannot shoot a basketball with proper form or throw a baseball correctly, but if I ask them to stickhandle through a puck maze and then pass five pucks into a bucket while on their inside edge, it isn't a problem. In my opinion, transferable skills are the key to any good athlete. It was fun as a kid to look forward to the upcoming baseball season after hockey was done. Then when soccer season wrapped up, I looked forward to getting back on the ice. Sports is meant to be fun, and by playing only one sport, the love of that game will eventually fade away. After all, these are kids we are talking about, not robots.

What has changed over the last couple of years in the game of hockey? Well, both retired and current hockey players have learned to communicate. From a young age we have been taught to stay quiet, know your role and play the game. The courage of Kyle Beach, Akim Aliu, and others to come forward has allowed players to open up with each other and with the media. I have had more candid conversations with friends, family, and former teammates in the last two years than during my entire hockey career. Through this dialogue with each other, previous generations of players have learned that not everything we have experienced was right. We have our own kids now, and watching them play the game brings up memories from our past. Not every memory is terrible, but it is our job to protect the next generation. When my dad found out that Daniel Carcillo was spearheading a class action lawsuit against the Canadian Hockey League and its member teams on behalf of former players who suffered abuse during their time in junior hockey, he texted me.

Dad: "Did you see the junior hockey story in the paper?"
Me: "Yup"
Dad: "What did you think?"
Me: "Unfortunately, that's the half of it, Dad"
Dad: "If I had known this went on, I would have never let you go. I hope the players win and force them to change. All management should be liable. We not only lost those years with you at home but we exposed you to these crimes."

He called them crimes, and for the first time in my life, I realized he was right. I wept — cried for an hour. Who am I protecting by staying silent? Former coaches and general managers climb the ladder of the hockey world, while we are left to process the impact of the decisions they made along the way. The pain that my parents feel knowing they left their son with negligent adults and the pain that I feel now cannot be forgotten. I don't want money from book sales, or class action lawsuits, and I am not out to destroy careers. I don't want publicity, but I know that some attention will come from this and I am prepared to talk about resolutions. I want parents to see what the game looks like to an average player and I want junior hockey to stop hiding the systemic issues that have been around for decades. *STOP.* Let's talk. I am no longer afraid of the blowback. I'm not perfect and I have witnessed things I should've stopped hundreds of times. I was led to believe that these things were normal within hockey culture.

Hockey culture: it's a commonly used phrase inside the game, and it's meant to glorify sacrifice, dedication, toughness, loyalty, and a sense of identity. Hockey culture is used as a term of endearment that an everyday civilian would never understand. I always viewed this "culture" as something exclusive that I was lucky enough to experience. Those on the outside didn't have the privilege, and they couldn't understand our world and the baggage that came with it. Unfortunately, when you step outside of the game for a long period of time, you begin to see the toxicity of that culture. When the moment of realization occured, when I finally understood that the world I dedicated my life to was full of racism, deviance, and bullying, it hit me like a brick. I began to understand that hockey had contributed to my disillusionment and altered reality. I needed to be fixed.

So when the allegations of Kyle Beach's sexual abuse were exposed, I believed him immediately.

I wasn't shocked. Instead, I was surprised the truth took so long to come out. I had friends, coworkers, and family ask, *Can you believe that this took place?* Of course I believe it. Hockey culture makes it possible, and it makes you believe that something like this is normal. Unchallenged, dictatorial, authoritarian power was rampant throughout my career, and it still exists today — just ask Kyle Beach. A common observation was: "Beach was six foot five and the abuser was five foot six, how did he let the abuse happen if he didn't want it to happen?" Power allows people to have absolute control over those who don't have it while also robbing the powerless of their voice.

Let me explain things through my lens, from the inside. Beach was a "Black Ace." That term "affectionately" refers to a player who is never going to play in a game or even be on the active roster but is skated extremely hard after practice throughout the playoffs. The goal of a Black Ace is to use their sacrifice and their passion to inspire the team. Their job is to shut up and do whatever a player in the lineup asks them to do. If they don't like it, the organization will find someone else to do it instead. In hockey culture, being a Black Ace is like wearing a badge of honour, as you are respected for being worn down both physically and mentally on a daily basis, and it is your first step to a career in the NHL. Does a 20-year-old Black Ace coming in from the WHL sound like someone who would have a voice in an organization that is a few steps away from a Stanley Cup? Of course not. The five-foot-six video coach had all of the power and the respect of the organization.

Who do you think the organization is going to believe?

I was listening to *Overdrive* in the car one afternoon, and the co-host, former NHL goalie Jamie McLennan, commented that, "Hockey is ninety-five percent amazing, but the five percent . . . there are serious issues there and they have to be dealt with." His statement hit home with me. When I try to wrap my head around the issues that come up time and time again, I can't ignore that a major factor in all of this is the clichéd but very real "old boys' network." What other sport immediately promotes a player to a general manager's role, an assistant general manager position, a player development job, or even a head scouting role because they were good at the game? Why does someone get looked at right away for a high ranking position without any experience because they were a good teammate or because they can be trusted? Martin St. Louis went from coaching minor hockey right into an NHL head coaching position, bypassing more qualified candidates who had devoted their entire life behind the bench. After all, he was a good player.

The old boys' network conceals serious issues behind closed doors because that is what a good teammate does. Hockey culture consists of protecting the organization at all costs. Where other sports demand that you start your management career in the minor leagues or that you start your career on the bottom rungs of the game when you retire, hockey often promotes those closest to the game into positions of power. These promotions and hires breed a sense of loyalty to those who hired you and to the closed culture and secrecy involved in McLennan's 5 percent. Would you ignore serious allegations and look the other way to protect the person who gave you a job with a $200,000 salary and that you're unqualified for? Have a look at where the people who report these allegations, those who break the hockey code, end up. The game seems to find room for the rehabilitation of those who stay silent and forgets about those who do not. Taylor Hall, talking about Kyle Beach, said it best to reporters on the radio: "Every culture needs to keep getting better, and hockey's no different. This is a game that's a little bit of a, I guess what you would call, an old boys' club, and there's definitely some secrecy and things that need to change." He continued, "Hopefully they can. You never want to think of an incident like this . . . because it's been so terrible, but there needs to be changes, and unfortunately people need to be held accountable." Of course someone needs to be held accountable, but if everyone is tied together — part of an incestuous family tree — who is going to be the agent of change?

By writing about this issue and talking about my experiences, I will offend people. I will be called many things and my career will be dissected to show how I was soft . . . how I'm a nobody. Who is Justin Davis and why does his opinion even matter? People will hear my side of the story and see it very differently. I understand, I was one of those people, too, at one time. I viewed my time inside the game as a privilege and the one thing that defined who I was. I still value 75 percent of my time within the game of hockey and the positives that came with it. It wasn't until I had three kids, became a high school teacher, and began my evolution into "civilian" that I realized the system is broken. I loved my time in hockey and my teammates along the way. I cherish those memories and miss the dressing room every day. I would give anything to sit in my half equipment and banter for hours about nothing, but I am now here to help fix that 5 percent of hockey that has been broken for far too long. I don't want to read about another Kyle Beach.

When I sat down to watch the response by the only upper management person to remain unpunished after the Beach incident, Kevin Cheveldayoff, it was the final reminder of what needs to change. Before the incident was revealed, Cheveldayoff's resumé included assistant to the general manager and senior director of hockey operations with the Chicago Blackhawks during their Stanley Cup run. His role in the Stanley Cup run was invaluable. After the allegations surfaced that he was in a meeting where the sexual abuse incident was discussed, his role seemed to dissipate into that of a junior member of the management team and of someone without a voice. He couldn't speak up because nobody would listen to him as he was just a small spoke in the wheel of success. It's amazing how someone with multiple titles in senior management couldn't help a player who was sexually assaulted. Therefore, Cheveldayoff was absolved of all guilt and Stan Bowman was the fall guy for the franchise. But Bowman will be back in the game someday — I guarantee it. He will be rehabilitated by the code itself — by the fact that he took the blame for the team, by the fact that he is a true hockey guy. My opinion is that the majority of the people involved weren't sorry that it happened — they were sorry that their inaction was made public. Was it too hard to say sorry? Why couldn't Gary Bettman just say "I'm sorry it happened and I want to make sure it never happens again"? In writing this book, I know I will get my wrist slapped for breaking from hockey culture . . . and others will end our friendship altogether. How can I take Kyle Beach's side? How can I say the game is broken? How can I criticize a game that gave me so much? I can have this opinion because I agree with Jamie McLennan: I loved 95 percent of the game. I miss that part of it every day.

But the other 5 percent? That part has damaged me more than the 95 percent ever helped me. I'm tired of sitting back and waxing poetic about "our game." It's 2022 and players are still silent about abuse in the locker room, and the old boys' club still protects its own. And it has to stop.

I am thankful for many things during this process. I'm thankful for a family that supported me when I needed it. My brother and sister showed up to so many places on the road when I wanted to see my family badly.

I always put up a brave front like I was doing fine, but I was thankful for those moments. My mom and dad were put through the ringer. I had to move out unexpectedly at 16, I was arrested, suffered multiple injuries, and was traded two times. All of this had a huge impact on my entire family. Imagine watching your son get severely injured on the ice and then taken away quickly without knowing his condition. At least my parents believed I was receiving the proper medical care and, thankfully, they were always reassured that everything was perfectly fine. In reality, it never was. My mom would drive up a pair of dress shoes to Kingston if she thought I needed them or she would make an excuse to stop in. It became too much for my mom near the end of junior hockey, and it wasn't enjoyable for her to watch. She came to the games to see me and to ask if I needed anything. The joy of the game was lost on her as well. I understand it now as I deal with my own kids, and it's tough to see them going through adversity. My dad, on the other hand, came to everything. I started out each warm-up secretly trying to find him in the stands. When I found him in his usual perch, I could relax. Sometimes if I was playing terribly, Dad would leave after the second period because he started work at 5:30 a.m. I don't blame him. I remember our breakfasts at Harveys after my 6 a.m. practices in AAA. I remember long car rides as we sat in silence and listened to the radio, much like the car rides now with my own kids. Dad put up with a lot of crap over the years, and I'm understanding now why he always stood by himself. I'm grateful that my parents were always there for me whenever I needed them and that they provided me with anything I needed. New skates, sticks, and rep fees were always paid, even when times were tough and the money wasn't there. My family were my biggest fans, and although I didn't show it then, I am forever grateful.

Finally, I am only able to sit down and write all of this because of Jess. She came at the perfect time in my life, as most of the crap was finished. We entered a new phase of our life together, and I was lucky that I met her. We have grown together, and she has always been supportive of my career. We are coming up on 20 years married, and I can't imagine my life without her. Before I got married, I always pictured my wife as someone who:

1) was a Christian
2) was good looking
3) didn't run funny and could throw a spiral
4) had a sense of humour like mine
5) was a great mom to our kids

This is Jess. We are lucky to have three great kids who are each unique in their own way. Grace and Avery were born three years apart in Guelph, a couple of years after our return to Canada. Grace is a confident, athletic child with a heart of gold. She is extremely creative and loves to design anything to her liking. Avery is quiet and athletic as well. She is sensitive and cerebral with a sense of humour. Josh, unfortunately, is following in my footsteps, and I can see parts of myself in him each day. His athleticism, sense of humour, humble spirit, and fear of disappointment remind me of my younger days. I fear that I may have helped foster his lack of excitement over any major accomplishment. The girls are coming into their own and they are discovering sports as they get older. It brings me happiness to see them falling in love with soccer and packing their bags for practice. To see them improve daily and to see their excitement before practice is what sports is all about. It's not about making the top team or being the best player. It's about teammates, life lessons, adversity and, most of all, having fun. I'm proud of my kids and I'm glad that they are finding themselves in sports. My job is to make sure that I support them, I don't ruin the experience, and to tell them that I love them, no matter what happens. At the end of the day, isn't that why I signed up for hockey in the first place?

ACKNOWLEDGEMENTS

This memoir was written over the course of two years, during a global pandemic. Let's just say I had a lot of time on my hands. There were so many people who helped me along the way. From phone calls, to emails, to long in-person conversations with people from my past, I am forever indebted to everyone who played a part. I know I can't thank each and every person but here are a few people who played an integral part in this process.

Mom and Dad, what can I say to the two people who did their best to protect me and are reading these things for the very first time? It wasn't your fault. I am forever thankful for the unconditional love you showed me through my highs and lows, and the arrests and accomplishments. You were the best parents anyone could have asked for even though you didn't tell me our dog died during my second OHL season and I came home to a new puppy. I love you guys, and I know this can't be easy.

A huge thank you to my brother and sister for their support. Kyle, rehashing some of these stories for the book made me laugh until I cried. Your visits were a break from the monotony of the game and the protection only a big brother could provide. Thanks for providing some great stories and for being my biggest fan. Shannon, it's not until I started my memoir that I began realizing why certain people were put in my life. My sister was one of my best friends growing up and a vault for hiding all of my mistakes. Thanks for always having my back and being there when I needed you the most.

Many thanks to Neal Costello for being the VHS memory tape of my life. From my skinny buddy with the glasses down the road, to being my starting pitcher, right winger, and roommate. Nobody knew me better and could clarify the stories from this book. Your recall was outstanding and the microfiche of the research process. You encouraged me to keep going with this and offered me valuable feedback. Most importantly, you told me that I was a better player than what I gave myself credit for and that I wasn't average. That meant a lot. Your friendship with me means more than you'll ever know.

To the Stone family, I appreciate you accepting me and supporting me through this process. Sue was the first person to see my manuscript and she didn't say she hated it. It was the first step in making this a real thing.

A special thanks to Leticia Araujo for taking the time to generously volunteer with editing when this project was still in its early stages.

Much obliged to Brian Wood. Trust me, my Grade 12 English teacher would never have believed that I would have a literary agent. Thank you for believing in my story and accepting a submission from a rookie nobody. You championed my memoir and implored me to share my story. We met on the last day of normal life before the pandemic at Starbucks and it's been a wild two years since. Thank you for believing in me and finding me a publisher who cared, even when I had given up hope. You understood what this was from the very beginning. I also want to express my deepest gratitude to Michael Holmes, Shannon Parr, and Jessica Albert from ECW.

I knew nothing, absolutely nothing, about how a memoir was shaped and created. You walked me through this entire process with patience and made me feel like a part of the ECW family. Michael, I can't thank you enough for bringing me in and allowing me to tell my story. From our first phone call, I knew I was in good hands. Shannon, your organization and collaboration in the editing process made my original copy a whole lot better. Thank you for putting the finishing touches on everything. Jessica, the vision for the cover is something I will always be proud of. Thank you from the bottom of my heart. Also, to Heather Pollock, the photo day was one of my favourite parts of this process. You're awesome.

I appreciate the help from Allan Walsh, my third and final player agent. I wondered who this man was waiting for me after a game, wearing cowboy boots and a suit in the hall of the Kingston Memorial Centre. It turns out he would become my biggest advocate in the hockey world. I may not have lived up to my future potential, but you showed compassion and integrity while looking out for my best interests. I appreciate your help with clarifying and piecing together parts of my career for this book. I wanted to make sure that I got specific sections of this book perfect. I will be forever grateful to you for always answering the phone. Thanks for fighting for me.

Brian Kilrea, thank you for investing so much time into my life. You came into my world at my lowest moment, and I am the man I am today because of you. Thank you for helping with the foreword and allowing me to share some insight into the world of the 67's. When I called two years ago out of the blue, you picked up the phone on the second ring and talked to me like it was 1999 all over again. You and Judy made me feel important, and I will never forget that. I hope that this book paints the picture correctly. Likewise, a huge thank you to Jeff Hunt for your help with the stories in the book and allowing the 67's to be on the cover. It means a lot to me. You took over the franchise at the perfect time, and I thank you for making this book possible. Finally, Teresa Kelly, you made me enjoy school again and stoked the fires of reading and writing. This whole thing started in my mind 23 years ago. Ottawa still feels like family.

It's tough to thank a neighbourhood, but the Henderson Crew was a sounding board for me. At 2 a.m. on Friday nights, three buddies played darts in a cold garage and you would tell me my stories should be in a book. That was the beginning. Who said bad things happen after midnight?

Many thanks as well to Chris George. I appreciate you taking the time to answer my questions and to give me clarity into the topic of diversity in hockey. I wish I was a better teammate. Thank you for explaining to me that ignorance in the game isn't necessarily negative but once we are made aware of it and understand the problem, we need to be a part of the solution. This is my start. I especially want to thank all of my other former teammates who I reached out to in making sure that my memories were correct. You listened to me ramble on and provided feedback that was key to this book. I am thankful for your support in this process and for allowing me to use your names and stories. Going into battle each week and the banter in the dressing room is why I played the game. You reminded me of this. I'm sorry for not backchecking but I always had the high guy. Thanks to the Coalition, I guess I was wrong that I wouldn't make lifelong friends at Western. Thanks for supporting me with this and not making me feel weak when talking about mental health. You were a big part of my world on the ice, during the writing process, and during this important stage now. I know I will lean on your support after publication and your friendships mean the world to me.

Jess, what can I say? Thank you for being my writing partner, my editor, spellchecker, supporter and critic, publicist and friend. You like to refer to yourself as the "wordsmith" and I hate to admit it, but you are. This was a hard process for the both of us, but you gave me space when I needed it. You married me knowing my backstory and encouraged me to share my life with the world. I can't thank you enough for the work you did behind the scenes and for listening to all of my crazy thoughts and ideas. There were so many times that I needed a shoulder to cry on and you gave me the encouragement that this will actually facilitate positive discussion in the hockey world. I cannot thank you enough and if hockey did one thing right, it led me to you. I love you.

Justin Davis is a high school teacher and former professional hockey player. He was drafted 85th overall by the Washington Capitals in the 1996 NHL draft. After assisting on the overtime goal in the 1999 Memorial Cup, while leading the tournament in scoring, he went on to Western University. Justin was an assistant captain of the 2002 University Cup-winning team while completing his degree in Kinesiology and winning the prestigious Purple Blanket Award. He remains the all-time points leader at UWO. After a two-year stint in Germany, Justin wrapped up his hockey career by winning the 2014 Allan Cup with the Dundas Real McCoys, once again assisting on the overtime winner. He volunteers with the Guelph Storm in a player mentorship and chaplain position. Justin currently lives in Guelph, Ontario, with his wife, Jessie, and three kids, Josh, Grace, and Avery.

This book is also available as a Global Certified Accessible™ (GCA) ebook. ECW Press's ebooks are screen reader friendly and are built to meet the needs of those who are unable to read standard print due to blindness, low vision, dyslexia, or a physical disability.

At ECW Press, we want you to enjoy our books in whatever format you like. If you've bought a print copy, just send an email to ebook@ecwpress.com and include:

- the book title
- the name of the store where you purchased it
- a screenshot or picture of your order / receipt number and your name
- your preference of file type: PDF (for desktop reading), ePub (for a phone / tablet, Kobo, or Nook), mobi (for Kindle)

A real person will respond to your email with your ebook attached. Please note this offer is only for copies bought for personal use and does not apply to school or library copies.

Thank you for supporting an independently owned Canadian publisher with your purchase!

This book is made of paper from well-managed FSC® - certified forests, recycled materials, and other controlled sources.